Principles
in Practice

The Principles in Practice imprint offers teachers concrete illustrations of effective classroom practices based in NCTE research briefs and policy statements. Each book discusses the research on a specific topic, links the research to an NCTE brief or policy statement, and then demonstrates how those principles come alive in practice: by showcasing actual classroom practices that demonstrate the policies in action; by talking about research in practical, teacher-friendly language; and by offering teachers possibilities for rethinking their own practices in light of the ideas presented in the books. Books within the imprint are grouped in strands, each strand focused on a significant topic of interest.

Volumes in the Adolescent Literacy Strand

Adolescent Literacy at Risk? The Impact of Standards (2009) Rebecca Bowers Sipe

Adolescents and Digital Literacies: Learning Alongside Our Students (2010) Sara Kajder

Adolescent Literacy and the Teaching of Reading: Lessons for Teachers of Literature (2010) Deborah Appleman

Volumes in the Writing in Today's Classrooms Strand

Writing in the Dialogical Classroom: Students and Teachers Responding to the Texts of Their Lives (2011) Bob Fecho

Becoming Writers in the Elementary Classroom: Visions and Decisions (2011) Katie Van Sluys

Writing Instruction in the Culturally Relevant Classroom (2011) Maisha T. Winn and Latrise P. Johnson

Writing Instruction in the Culturally Relevant Classroom

Maisha T. Winn
Emory University

Latrise P. Johnson
Emory University

National Council of Teachers of English
1111 W. Kenyon Road, Urbana, Illinois 61801-1096

Manuscript Editor: Lisa McAvoy

Staff Editor: Bonny Graham

Imprint Editor: Cathy Fleischer

Interior Design: Victoria Pohlmann

Cover Design: Pat Mayer

NCTE Stock Number: 58562

Library of Congress Cataloging-in-Publication Data

Winn, Maisha T.
    Writing instruction in the culturally relevant classroom / Maisha T. Winn, Latrise P. Johnson.
        p. cm.
    Includes biliographical references and index.
    ISBN 978-0-8141-5856-2 (pbk)
  1. Composition (Language arts)—Study and teaching (Secondary)—United States.
2. Multiculturalism—United States. I. Johnson, Latrise P. II. Title.
    LB1631.W56 2011
    808'.0420712—dc23
                                                    2011035726

To our students who shared their lives with us through writing.

To our fellow teachers who worked with us to develop critical thinkers, readers, and writers.

Contents

Acknowledgments

We would like to acknowledge Cathy Fleischer for her patience, excellent feedback, and pushing that felt more like a loving nudge. Cathy's effort to create a series that speaks directly to teachers is fueled with passion and commitment. Her enthusiasm is infectious and we delighted in the opportunity to work closely with her on this project.

Many, many thanks go to Ariah Bashir, Latrise's daughter, and Obasi Winn, Maisha's son, who put up with our writing meetings. Ariah diligently worked on homework, read books, and ate dinner quietly while we toiled over word choice and voice, while Obasi hung out with Dad or "dee-jayed" in his play dee-jay booth. Ariah and Obasi are the reasons we do this work; they are our future and when we look at them, we see the world in all its possibilities.

Lawrence "Torry" Winn, Maisha's husband, has been one of our biggest exhorters. Whether he was working at the same café at another table so we could meet or quietly reading in another room while we discussed directions for the manuscript, he was always present in whatever capacity we needed him to be.

Denise Thomas, Latrise's twin sister, has been very supportive through this process. We thank her for listening and offering invaluable feedback. We also thank her for being an exceptional educator with whom we can share, debate, and grow.

Cultivating New Voices scholars, past and present, provide constant inspiration and support.

The Division of Educational Studies at Emory University, one of our intellectual homes, provided a safe space to do our work. We thank all of our colleagues and friends throughout the university community who encouraged us along the way.

NCTE Beliefs about the Teaching of Writing

Just as the nature of and expectation for literacy has changed in the past century and a half, so has the nature of writing. Much of that change has been due to technological developments, from pen and paper, to typewriter, to word processor, to networked computer, to design software capable of composing words, images, and sounds. These developments not only expanded the types of texts that writers produce, they also expanded immediate access to a wider variety of readers. With full recognition that writing is an increasingly multifaceted activity, we offer several principles that should guide effective teaching practice.

Everyone has the capacity to write, writing can be taught, and teachers can help students become better writers

Though poets and novelists may enjoy debating whether or not writing can be taught, teachers of writing have more pragmatic aims. Setting aside the question of whether one can learn to be an artistic genius, there is ample empirical evidence that anyone can get better at writing, and that what teachers do makes a difference in how much students are capable of achieving as writers.

Developing writers require support. This support can best come through carefully designed writing instruction oriented toward acquiring new strategies and skills. Certainly, writers can benefit from teachers who simply support and give them time to write. However, instruction matters. Teachers of writing should be well-versed in composition theory and research, and they should know methods for turning that theory into practice. When writing teachers first walk into classrooms, they should already know and practice good composition. However, much as in doctoring, learning to teach well is a lifetime process, and lifetime professional development is the key to successful practice. Students deserve no less.

People learn to write by writing

As is the case with many other things people do, getting better at writing requires doing it—a lot. This means actual writing, not merely listening to lectures about writing, doing grammar drills, or discussing readings. The more people write, the easier it gets and the more they are motivated to do it. Writers who write a lot learn more about the process because they have had more experience inside it. Writers learn from each session with their hands on a keyboard or around a pencil as they draft, rethink, revise, and draft again. Thinking about how to make your writing better is what revision is. In other words, improvement is built into the experience of writing.

What does this mean for teaching?

Writing instruction must include ample in-class and out-of-class opportunities for writing and should include writing for a variety of purposes and audiences.

Writing, though, should not be viewed as an activity that happens only within a classroom's walls. Teachers need to support students in the development of writing lives, habits,

NCTE Beliefs about the Teaching of Writing

and preferences for life outside school. We already know that many students do extensive amounts of self-sponsored writing: emailing, keeping journals or doing creative projects, instant messaging, making Web sites, blogging, and so on. As much as possible, instruction should be geared toward making sense in a life outside of school, so that writing has ample room to grow in individuals' lives. It is useful for teachers to consider what elements of their curriculum they could imagine students self-sponsoring outside of school. Ultimately, those are the activities that will produce more writing.

In order to provide quality opportunities for student writing, teachers must minimally understand:

- How to interpret curriculum documents, including things that can be taught while students are actually writing, rather than one thing at a time to all students at once.
- The elements of "writing lives" as people construct them in the world outside of school.
- Social structures that support independent work.
- How to confer with individual writers.
- How to assess while students are writing.
- How to plan what students need to know in response to ongoing research.
- How to create a sense of personal safety in the classroom, so that students are willing to write freely and at length.
- How to create community while students are writing in the same room together.

Writing is a process

Often, when people think of writing, they think of texts—finished pieces of writing. Understanding what writers do, however, involves thinking not just about what texts look like when they are finished but also about what strategies writers might employ to produce those texts. Knowledge about writing is only complete with understanding the complex of actions in which writers engage as they produce texts. Such understanding has two aspects. First is the development, through extended practice over years, of a repertory of routines, skills, strategies, and practices for generating, revising, and editing different kinds of texts. Second is the development of reflective abilities and meta-awareness about writing. This procedural understanding helps writers most when they encounter difficulty, or when they are in the middle of creating a piece of writing. How does someone get started? What do they do when they get stuck? How do they plan the overall process, each section of their work, and even the rest of the sentence they are writing right now? Research, theory, and practice over the past 40 years has produced a richer understanding of what writers do—those who are proficient and professional as well as those who struggle.

Two further points are vital. To say that writing is a process is decidedly not to say that it should—or can—be turned into a formulaic set of steps. Experienced writers shift between different operations according to tasks and circumstances. Second, writers do not accumulate process skills and strategies once and for all. They develop and refine writing skills throughout their writing lives.

NCTE Beliefs about the Teaching of Writing

What does this mean for teaching?

Whenever possible, teachers should attend to the process that students might follow to produce texts—and not only specify criteria for evaluating finished products, in form or content. Students should become comfortable with prewriting techniques, multiple strategies for developing and organizing a message, a variety of strategies for revising and editing, and strategies for preparing products for public audiences and for deadlines. In explaining assignments, teachers should provide guidance and options for ways of going about it. Sometimes, evaluating the processes students follow—the decisions they make, the attempts along the way—can be as important as evaluating the final product. At least some of the time, the teacher should guide the students through the process, assisting them as they go. Writing instruction must provide opportunities for students to identify the processes that work best for themselves as they move from one writing situation to another.

Writing instruction must also take into account that a good deal of workplace writing and other writing takes place in collaborative situations. Writers must learn to work effectively with one another.

Teachers need to understand at least the following in order to be excellent at teaching writing as a process:

- The relationship between features of finished writing and the actions writers perform.
- What writers of different genres say about their craft.
- The process of writing from the inside, that is, what they themselves as writers experience in a host of different writing situations.
- Multiple strategies for approaching a wide range of typical problems writers face during composing, including strategies for audience and task analysis, invention, revision, and editing.
- Multiple models of the writing process, the varied ways individuals approach similar tasks, and the ways that writing situations and genres inform processes.
- Published texts, immediately available, that demonstrate a wide range of writing strategies and elements of craft.
- The relationships among the writing process, curriculum, learning, and pedagogy.
- How to design time for students to do their best work on an assignment.
- How writers use tools, including word-processing and design software and computer-based resources.

Writing is a tool for thinking

When writers actually write, they think of things that they did not have in mind before they began writing. The act of writing generates ideas. This is different from the way we often think of writers—as getting ideas fixed in their heads before they write them down. The notion that writing is a medium for thought is important in several ways. It suggests a number of important uses for writing: to solve problems, to identify issues, to construct questions, to

NCTE Beliefs about the Teaching of Writing

reconsider something one had already figured out, to try out a half-baked idea. This insight that writing is a tool for thinking helps us to understand the process of drafting and revision as one of exploration and discovery, and is nothing like transcribing from prerecorded tape. The writing process is not one of simply fixing up the mistakes in an early draft, but of finding more and more wrinkles and implications in what one is talking about.

What does this mean for teaching?

In any writing classroom, some of the writing is for others and some of the writing is for the writer. Regardless of the age, ability, or experience of the writer, the use of writing to generate thought is still valuable; therefore, forms of writing such as personal narrative, journals, written reflections, observations, and writing-to-learn strategies are important.

In any writing assignment, it must be assumed that part of the work of writers will involve generating and regenerating ideas prior to writing them.

Excellence in teaching writing as thinking requires that the teacher understand:

- Varied tools for thinking through writing, such as journals, writers' notebooks, blogs, sketchbooks, digital portfolios, listservs or online discussion groups, dialogue journals, double-entry or dialectical journals, and others.
- The kinds of new thinking that occur when writers revise.
- The variety of types of thinking people do when they compose, and what those types of thinking look like when they appear in writing.
- Strategies for getting started with an idea, or finding an idea when one does not occur immediately.

Writing grows out of many different purposes

Purposes for writing include developing social networks; engaging in civic discourse; supporting personal and spiritual growth; reflecting on experience; communicating professionally and academically; building relationships with others, including friends, family, and like-minded individuals; and engaging in aesthetic experiences.

Writing is not just one thing. It varies in form, structure, and production process according to its audience and purpose. A note to a cousin is not like a business report, which is different again from a poem. The processes and ways of thinking that lead up to these varied kinds of texts can also vary widely, from the quick single-draft email to a friend to the careful drafting and redrafting of a legal contract. The different purposes and forms both grow out of and create various relationships between the writer and the potential reader, and relationships reflected in degrees of formality in language, as well as assumptions about what knowledge and experience is already shared, and what needs to be explained. Writing with certain purposes in mind, the writer focuses her attention on what the audience is thinking or believing; other times, the writer focuses more on the information she is organizing, or on her own thoughts and feelings. Therefore, the thinking, the procedures, and the physical format in writing all differ when writers' purposes vary.

NCTE Beliefs about the Teaching of Writing

What does this mean for teaching?

Often, in school, students write only to prove that they did something they were asked to do, in order to get credit for it. Or, students are taught a single type of writing and are led to believe this type will suffice in all situations. Writers outside of school have many different purposes beyond demonstrating accountability, and they practice myriad types and genres. In order to make sure students are learning how writing differs when the purpose and the audience differ, it is important that teachers create opportunities for students to be in different kinds of writing situations, where the relationships and agendas are varied. Even within academic settings, the characteristics of good writing vary among disciplines; what counts as a successful lab report, for example, differs from a successful history paper, essay exam, or literary interpretation.

In order to teach for excellence about purposes in writing, teachers need to understand:

- The wide range of purposes for which people write, and the forms of writing that arise from those purposes.
- Strategies and forms for writing for public participation in a democratic society.
- Ways people use writing for personal growth, expression, and reflection, and how to encourage and develop this kind of writing.
- Aesthetic or artistic forms of writing and how they are made. That is, the production of creative and literary texts, for the purposes of entertainment, pleasure, or exploration.
- Appropriate forms for varied academic disciplines and the purposes and relationships that create those forms.
- Ways of organizing and transforming school curricula in order to provide students with adequate education in varied purposes for writing.
- How to set up a course to write for varied purposes and audiences.

Conventions of finished and edited texts are important to readers and therefore to writers

Readers expect writing to conform to their expectations, to match the conventions generally established for public texts. Contemporary readers expect words to be spelled in a standardized way, for punctuation to be used in predictable ways, for usage and syntax to match that used in texts they already acknowledge as successful. They expect the style in a piece of writing to be appropriate to its genre and social situation. In other words, it is important that writing that goes public be "correct."

What does this mean for teaching?

Every teacher has to resolve a tension between writing as generating and shaping ideas and writing as demonstrating expected surface conventions. On the one hand, it is important for writing to be as correct as possible and for students to be able to produce correct texts. On the other hand, achieving correctness is only one set of things writers must be able to do; a correct text empty of ideas or unsuited to its audience or purpose is not a good piece

NCTE Beliefs about the Teaching of Writing

of writing. There is no formula for resolving this tension. Writing is both/and: both fluency and fitting conventions. Research shows that facility in these two operations often develops unevenly. For example, as students learn increasingly sophisticated ways of thinking (for example, conditional or subordinate reasoning) or dealing with unfamiliar content, they may produce more surface errors, or perhaps even seem to regress. This is because their mental energies are focused on the new intellectual challenges. Such uneven development is to be tolerated, in fact, encouraged. It is rather like strength gains from lifting weight, which actually tears down muscle fibers only to stimulate them to grow back stronger. Too much emphasis on correctness can actually inhibit development. By the same token, without mastering conventions for written discourse, writers' efforts may come to naught. Drawing readers' attention to the gap between the text at hand and the qualities of texts they expect causes readers to not attend to the content. Each teacher must be knowledgeable enough about the entire landscape of writing instruction to guide particular students toward a goal, developing both increasing fluency in new contexts and mastery of conventions. NCTE's stated policy over many years has been that conventions of writing are best taught in the context of writing. Simply completing workbook or online exercises is inadequate if students are not regularly producing meaningful texts themselves.

Most writing teachers teach students how to edit their writing that will go out to audiences. This is often considered a late stage in the process of composing, because editing is only essential for the words that are left after all the cutting, replacing, rewriting, and adding that go on during revision. Writers need an image in their minds of conventional grammar, spelling, and punctuation in order to compare what is already on the page to an ideal of correctness. They also need to be aware of stylistic options that will produce the most desirable impression on their readers. All of the dimensions of editing are motivated by a concern for an audience.

Teachers should be familiar with techniques for teaching editing and encouraging reflective knowledge about editing conventions. For example, some find it useful to have students review a collection of their writing over time—a journal, notebook, folder, or portfolio—to study empirically the way their writing has changed or needs to change, with respect to conventions. A teacher might say, "Let's look at all the times you used commas," or "Investigate the ways you might have combined sentences." Such reflective appointments permit students to set goals for their own improvement.

Teachers need to understand at least the following in order to be excellent at teaching conventions to writers:

- Research on developmental factors in writing ability, including the tension between fluency with new operations or contents and the practice of accepted spelling, punctuation, syntactic, and usage conventions.
- The diverse influences and constraints on writers' decision making as they determine the kinds of conventions that apply to this situation and this piece of writing.
- A variety of applications and options for most conventions.
- The appropriate conventions for academic classroom English.
- How to teach usage without excessive linguistic terminology.

NCTE Beliefs about the Teaching of Writing

- The linguistic terminology that is necessary for teaching particular kinds of usage.
- The linguistic terminology necessary for communicating professionally with other educators.
- The relationship among rhetorical considerations and decisions about conventions, for example, the conditions under which a dash, a comma, a semicolon, or a full stop might be more effective.
- Conventions beyond the sentence, such as effective uses of bulleted lists, mixed genres and voices, diagrams and charts, design of pages, and composition of video shots.
- An understanding of the relationship among conventions in primary and secondary discourses.
- The conditions under which people learn to do new things with language.
- The relationship between fluency, clarity, and correctness in writing development and the ability to assess which is the leading edge of the student's learning now.

Writing and reading are related

Writing and reading are related. People who read a lot have a much easier time getting better at writing. In order to write a particular kind of text, it helps if the writer has read that kind of text. In order to take on a particular style of language, the writer needs to have read that language, to have heard it in her mind, so that she can hear it again in order to compose it.

Writing can also help people become better readers. In their earliest writing experiences, children listen for the relationships of sounds to letters, which contributes greatly to their phonemic awareness and phonics knowledge. Writers also must learn how texts are structured, because they have to create them. The experience of plotting a short story, organizing a research report, or making line breaks in a poem permits the writer, as a reader, to approach new reading experiences with more informed eyes.

Additionally, reading is a vital source of information and ideas. For writers fully to contribute to a given topic or to be effective in a given situation, they must be familiar with what previous writers have said. Reading also creates a sense of what one's audience knows or expects on a topic.

What does this mean for teaching?

One way to help students become better writers is to make sure they have lots of extended time to read, in school and out. Most research indicates that the easiest way to tap motivation to read is to teach students to choose books and other texts they understand and enjoy, and then to give them time in school to read them. In addition to making students stronger readers, this practice makes them stronger writers.

Students should also have access to and experience in reading material that presents both published and student writing in various genres. Through immersion in a genre, students develop an internalized sense of why an author would select a particular genre for a particular purpose, the power of a particular genre to convey a message, and the rhetorical

NCTE Beliefs about the Teaching of Writing

constraints and possibilities inherent in a genre. Students should be taught the features of different genres, experientially not only explicitly, so that they develop facilities in producing them and become familiar with variant features. If one is going to write in a genre, it is very helpful to have read in that genre first.

Overall, frequent conversations about the connections between what we read and what we write are helpful. These connections will sometimes be about the structure and craft of the writing itself, and sometimes about thematic and content connections.

In order to do an excellent job of teaching into the connections of writing and reading, teachers need to understand at least these things:

- How writers read in a special way, with an eye toward not just what the text says but how it is put together.
- The psychological and social processes reading and writing have in common.
- The ways writers form and use constructs of their intended readers, anticipating their responses and needs.
- An understanding of text structure that is fluid enough to accommodate frequent disruptions.

Writing has a complex relationship to talk

From its beginnings in early childhood through the most complex setting imaginable, writing exists in a nest of talk. Conversely, speakers usually write notes and, regularly, scripts, and they often prepare visual materials that include texts and images. Writers often talk in order to rehearse the language and content that will go into what they write, and conversation often provides an impetus or occasion for writing. They sometimes confer with teachers and other writers about what to do next, how to improve their drafts, or in order to clarify their ideas and purposes. Their usual ways of speaking sometimes do and sometimes do not feed into the sentences they write, depending on an intricate set of decisions writers make continually. One of the features of writing that is most evident and yet most difficult to discuss is the degree to which it has "voice." The fact that we use this term, even in the absence of actual sound waves, reveals some of the special relationship between speech and writing.

What does this mean for teaching?

In early writing, we can expect lots of talk to surround writing, since what children are doing is figuring out how to get speech onto paper. Early teaching in composition should also attend to helping children get used to producing language orally, through telling stories, explaining how things work, predicting what will happen, and guessing about why things and people are the way they are. Early writing experiences will include students explaining orally what is in a text, whether it is printed or drawn.

As they grow, writers still need opportunities to talk about what they are writing about, to rehearse the language of their upcoming texts, and to run ideas by trusted colleagues before taking the risk of committing words to paper. After making a draft, it is often helpful for writers to discuss with peers what they have done, partly in order to get ideas from their peers, partly to see what they, the writers, say when they try to explain their thinking. Writing conferences, wherein student writers talk about their work with a teacher, who can make suggestions or re-orient what the writer is doing, are also very helpful uses of talk in the writing process.

To take advantage of the strong relationships between talk and writing, teachers must minimally understand:

- Ways of setting up and managing student talk in partnerships and groups.
- Ways of establishing a balance between talk and writing in classroom management.
- Ways of organizing the classroom and/or schedule to permit individual teacher-student conferences.
- Strategies for deliberate insertions of opportunities for talk into the writing process: knowing when and how students should talk about their writing.
- Ways of anticipating and solving interpersonal conflicts that arise when students discuss writing.
- Group dynamics in classrooms.
- Relationships—both similarities and differences—between oral and literate language.
- The uses of writing in public presentations and the values of students making oral presentations that grow out of and use their writing.

Literate practices are embedded in complicated social relationships

Writing happens in the midst of a web of relationships. There is, most obviously, the relationship between the writer and the reader. That relationship is often very specific: writers have a definite idea of who will read their words, not just a generalized notion that their text will be available to the world. Furthermore, particular people surround the writer—other writers, partners in purposes, friends, members of a given community—during the process of composing. They may know what the writer is doing and be indirectly involved in it, though they are not the audience for the work. In workplace and academic settings, writers write because someone in authority tells them to. Therefore, power relationships are built into the writing situation. In every writing situation, the writer, the reader, and all relevant others live in a structured social order, where some people's words count more than others, where being heard is more difficult for some people than others, where some people's words come true and others' do not.

Writers start in different places. It makes a difference what kind of language a writer spoke while growing up, and what kinds of language they are being asked to take on later in their experience. It makes a difference, too, the culture a writer comes from, the ways people use language in that culture, and the degree to which that culture is privileged in the larger society. Important cultural differences are not only ethnic but also racial, economic, geographical, and ideological. For example, rural students from small communities will have different language experiences than suburban students from comprehensive high schools, and students who come from very conservative backgrounds in which certain texts

NCTE Beliefs about the Teaching of Writing

are privileged or excluded will have different language experiences than those from progressive backgrounds in which the same is true. How much a writer has access to wide, diverse experiences and means of communication creates predispositions and skill for composing for an audience.

What does this mean for teaching?

The teaching of writing should assume students will begin with the sort of language with which they are most at home and most fluent in their speech. That language may be a dialect of English, or even a different language altogether. The goal is not to leave students where they are, however, but to move them toward greater flexibility, so that they can write not just for their own intimates but for wider audiences. Even as they move toward more widely used English, it is not necessary or desirable to wipe out the ways their family and neighborhood of origin use words. The teaching of excellence in writing means adding language to what already exists, not subtracting. The goal is to make more relationships available, not fewer.

In order to teach for excellence, a writing teacher needs understandings like these about contexts of language:

- How to find out about students' language use in the home and neighborhoods, the changes in language context they may have encountered in their lives, and the kinds of language they most value.
- That wider social situations in which students write, speak, read, and relate to other people affect what seems "natural" or "easy" to them—or not. How to discuss with students the need for flexibility in the employment of different kinds of language for different social contexts.
- How to help students negotiate maintenance of their most familiar language while mastering academic classroom English and the varieties of English used globally.
- Control and awareness of their own varied languages and linguistic contexts.
- An understanding of the relationships among group affiliation, identity, and language.
- Knowledge of the usual patterns of common dialects in English, such as African American English, Spanish and varieties of English related to Spanish, common patterns in American rural and urban populations, predictable patterns in the English varieties of groups common in their teaching contexts.
- How and why to study a community's ways of using language.

Composing occurs in different modalities and technologies

Increasingly rapid changes in technologies mean that composing is involving a combination of modalities, such as print, still images, video, and sound. Computers make it possible for these modalities to combine in the same work environment. Connections to the Internet not only make a range of materials available to writers, they also collapse distances between writers and readers and between generating words and creating designs. Print always has a visual component, even if it is only the arrangement of text on a page and the type font.

NCTE Beliefs about the Teaching of Writing

Furthermore, throughout history, print has often been partnered with pictures in order to convey more meaning, to add attractiveness, and to appeal to a wider audience. Television, video, and film all involve such combinations, as do websites and presentation software. As basic tools for communicating expand to include modes beyond print alone, "writing" comes to mean more than scratching words with pen and paper. Writers need to be able to think about the physical design of text, about the appropriateness and thematic content of visual images, about the integration of sound with a reading experience, and about the medium that is most appropriate for a particular message, purpose, and audience.

What does this mean for teaching?

Writing instruction must accommodate the explosion in technology from the world around us.

From the use of basic word processing to support drafting, revision, and editing to the use of hypertext and the infusion of visual components in writing, the definition of what writing instruction includes must evolve to embrace new requirements.

Many teachers and students do not, however, have adequate access to computing, recording, and video equipment to take advantage of the most up-to-date technologies. In many cases, teaching about the multimodal nature of writing is best accomplished through varying the forms of writing with more ordinary implements. Writing picture books allows students to think between text and images, considering the ways they work together and distribute the reader's attention. Similar kinds of visual/verbal thinking can be supported through other illustrated text forms, including some kinds of journals/sketchbooks and posters. In addition, writing for performance requires the writer to imagine what the audience will see and hear and thus draws upon multiple modes of thinking, even in the production of a print text. Such uses of technology without the latest equipment reveal the extent to which "new" literacies are rooted also in older ones.

Teachers need to understand at least the following in order to be excellent at teaching composition as involving multiple media:

- A range of new genres that have emerged with the increase in electronic communication. Because these genres are continually evolving, this knowledge must be continually updated.
- Operation of some of the hardware and software their students will use, including resources for solving software and hardware problems.
- Internet resources for remaining up to date on technologies.
- Design principles for webpages.
- Email and chat conventions.
- How to navigate both the World Wide Web and Web-based databases.
- The use of software for making websites, including basic html, such as how to make a link.
- Theory about the relationship between print and other modalities.

NCTE Beliefs about the Teaching of Writing

Assessment of writing involves complex, informed, human judgment

Assessment of writing occurs for different purposes. Sometimes, a teacher assesses in order to decide what the student has achieved and what he or she still needs to learn. Sometimes, an entity beyond the classroom assesses a student's level of achievement in order to say whether they can go on to some new educational level that requires the writer to be able to do certain things. At other times, school authorities require a writing test in order to pressure teachers to teach writing. Still other times, as in a history exam, the assessment of writing itself is not the point, but the quality of the writing is evaluated almost in passing. In any of these assessments of writing, complex judgments are formed. Such judgments should be made by human beings, not machines. Furthermore, they should be made by professionals who are informed about writing, development, and the field of literacy education.

What does this mean for teaching?

Instructors of composition should know about various methods of assessment of student writing. Instructors must recognize the difference between formative and summative evaluation and be prepared to evaluate students' writing from both perspectives. By formative evaluation here, we mean provisional, ongoing, in-process judgments about what students know and what to teach next. By summative evaluation, we mean final judgments about the quality of student work. Teachers of writing must also be able to recognize the developmental aspects of writing ability and devise appropriate lessons for students at all levels of expertise.

Teachers need to understand at least the following in order to be excellent at writing assessment:

- How to find out what student writers can do, informally, on an ongoing basis.
- How to use that assessment in order to decide what and how to teach next.
- How to assess occasionally, less frequently than above, in order to form judgments about the quality of student writing and learning.
- How to assess ability and knowledge across multiple writing engagements.
- What the features of good writing are, appropriate to the context and purposes of the teaching and learning.
- What the elements of a constructive process of writing are, appropriate to the context and purposes of the teaching and learning.

NCTE Beliefs about the Teaching of Writing

- What growth in writing looks like, the developmental aspects of writing ability.
- Ways of assessing student metacognitive process of the reading/writing connection.
- How to recognize in student writing (both in their texts and in their actions) the nascent potential for excellence at the features and processes desired.
- How to deliver useful feedback, appropriate for the writer and the situation.
- How to analyze writing situations for their most essential elements, so that assessment is not of everything about writing all at once, but rather is targeted to objectives.
- How to analyze and interpret both qualitative and quantitative writing assessments.
- How to evaluate electronic texts.
- How to use portfolios to assist writers in their development.
- How self-assessment and reflection contribute to a writer's development and ability to move among genres, media, and rhetorical situations.

A guideline by the Writing Study Group of the NCTE Executive Committee, November 2004

From Mis-education to Re-education: Our Journey

Latrise's Journey

When my twin sister, Denise, and I played school, it was a considerable production. We rounded up dolls and stuffed animals and gave them names to include
on a class roll. We collected pencils, pens, paper, and created miniature versions
of spelling, math, English, social studies, and science books, taking the time to
include questions or problems on each page for our "students" to complete. We
gathered books to read to them, thought of songs to sing, and even planned
what to have for lunch. Only after we were prepared did we line the "students"
up and commence to transform our bedroom into a classroom. I wanted to be
a teacher. I loved the idea of school and wanted to have a desk stacked with
paper, read books to eager listeners, and draw smiley faces on students' papers.
I was nine years old then and, as I reflect on my own schooling and the make-
believe schooling that was happening in the bedroom I shared with my sister, I
can remember having fun in both spaces. However, as I transitioned to middle
and high school, my experiences shifted, school changed, and I departed from
my childhood dream of becoming a teacher.

My middle and high school experiences were mediocre, to say the least. From the teachers to the lessons, nothing stands out to me as being particularly meaningful or memorable. For most of my secondary education, I sat quietly at my desk, completed assignments on worksheets or from textbooks, and was passed along without really being let in on the joke that was supposed to be my education. After that rather uninspiring middle school and high school experience, I attended Morris Brown College, where my desire to teach was reignited. My first year, I remember reading and discussing Toni Morrison's *The Bluest Eye*, and listening to my English 101 professor talk about the novel. I was captivated. We discussed a little black girl, Pecola Breedlove, with an abusive father and an indifferent mother who had to go and live with friends because her family was "put out." I remember asking myself, "Why didn't we read stuff like this in high school?" That is, books with little black girls in them who struggled with some of the same things I struggled with, or those that were set in places where I had been. Perhaps, if the teacher had provided literature that I connected with, maybe I would have finished a novel, participated more, or even earned better grades. I was inspired in my college English and literature classes to teach literature to students in a way that would help them connect to the writings in books and have a more meaningful and rich learning experience—one that would be the opposite of my own. There was a longing inside me to hear the voices and experiences from the literature that followed me after high school, one that inspired me to include culturally relevant pedagogy in my own classroom.

I was hired in Southeastern Urban District[1] at a time when there was an influx of scripted reading and math programs and classroom management initiatives, and when the Core Curriculum Tenets (CCT) were being replaced with State Performance Standards (SPS). There was limited acknowledgment of culturally relevant pedagogy and teaching. Instead, I was bombarded with professional development workshops, meetings, and seminars that centered on increasing student achievement through standardized testing. At the time, there was an increase in accountability discourse at every turn. While this accountability discourse played like a song on repeat in the corners of my mind, I was a new teacher with a desire to offer my students something I had not experienced as a student. I wanted students in this large urban school district that housed elementary, middle, and high schools to have a fun, meaningful education. I wanted my students to relate to the literature I taught and the writing I assigned. Little did I know that I would in many ways look back to my childhood to tap two of the most important skills that Denise and I practiced for hours as children in our classroom—planning and preparation—in order to create and present relevant, meaningful, and fun lessons to middle and high school students fifteen years later.

Perhaps one of the most memorable curricular units that I created as a public school teacher was a unit on poetry for ninth graders at Ellis High School. A great deal of planning went into this particular unit because I wanted my students to be able to connect with the content as well as find value in the activities related to learning poetic elements. In my previous experiences I found that students were not always receptive to concepts related to poetry despite the fact that they lived poetry daily through the tongues of their mothers, music in their headphones, and rhythms of their cosmopolitan city.

While brainstorming for this unit, I thought about how I could get the students in this school—more than 90 percent African American students and urban dwellers—interested in poetry. What would happen, I wondered, if I included some of that poetry of their lives, specifically songs and raps, alongside the poetry that was suggested by the state? As I began to plan, I searched for those songs and raps as well as many of my personal favorites gathered from poetry books I had around my house and choice picks from the bookstore. And when I thought about what to do for the unit project, one of my own college textbooks, *The Norton Anthology of Poetry*, inspired me; I decided to engage the young people in my ninth-grade literature class in creating their own anthology of poetry. This inquiry-driven project would allow students to explore different forms of poetry as well as connect with poems by numerous writers related to a variety of content. Perhaps most important, I would have an opportunity to learn from their "funds of knowledge" (González, Moll, & Amante, 2005) and experience what was important to them.

I started by introducing one of my favorite songs, Lauryn Hill's "The Mis-education of Lauryn Hill" (1998), to introduce poetic elements to the class. I found lyrics to the song in *Powerful Words: More Than 200 Years of Extraordinary Writing by African Americans* (Hudson, 2004), a book that featured these coveted lyrics from my generation. Coupled with the fact that I wanted a variety of texts in my classroom that featured African American writers—both historical and contemporary—I purchased the text for the beautiful sketches of featured writers illustrated by Marian Wright Edelman. (I copied, laminated, framed, and hung each portrait in the classroom.) I read the poem/lyrics to the students first and together we listened to the song on CD. After a second listening, we analyzed its content and structure.

As I assigned the poetry anthology project, I explained to the students that they would encounter many poems over the next few weeks and would compile a collection in their very own anthology. And I was amazed to discover how receptive my students were to reading and researching poetry on their own. As a part of the unit, we read and discussed many poems, rap and song lyrics, and a novel entitled *Love That Dog* by Sharon Creech. Students used the Internet as well as resources from the class library to collect material for their anthologies. Some students included original pieces they created for other assignments during the unit. A small fraction of class time was provided for students to conduct research for their anthologies; however, most was spent engaging classic and contemporary poets, listening to lyrics, discussing form and poetic elements, and sharing.

The poetry unit sparked something in me as well. I realized that while many of my lessons throughout my teaching journey had been good, this unit was different. Not only was it student-centered and inquiry-driven, the students could relate to the content they had to learn. I wanted to ensure they learned poetic elements, read a few poems, and, most important, discovered at least one thing about poetry that inspired them. Through this lesson, my students connected with a poet, a poem, or even a line of poetry that they found relevant to their lives.

Maisha's Journey

A familiar melody lured me into Latrise's ninth-grade literature class at Ellis High School. I agreed to work with classroom teachers in this small learning community (SLC) in the urban southeast. My role was to support teachers in their efforts to integrate inquiry into their curriculum and provide students with meaningful writing opportunities. As I got closer to the classroom where the music was playing, I quickly recognized the voice of singer-songwriter Lauryn Hill. When I peeked in the doorway, I was welcomed and ushered to a seat by Latrise. Students barely noticed me as they sat still, listening to the song. Secretly, I was thrilled to see students engaged in a song I considered to be a part of my generation's music since I found myself having to work harder to stay current with the new musical trends. After one listening, Latrise handed out copies of the lyrics to "The Miseducation of Lauryn Hill" from her album sharing this title. "This is one of my favorite songs," Latrise declared while holding up a book entitled *Powerful Words: More Than 200 Years of Extraordinary Writing by African Americans* (Hudson, 2004) featuring Hill's lyrics alongside famous poems, speeches, and other texts. After the second listening with lyrics in hand, Latrise asked her students to explicate the lyrics and discuss the literary devices when and where relevant. It would have been difficult not to notice that all of Latrise's students were African American and mostly male, especially given American public schools' well-documented failure to support black children, and boys in particular, academically (Irvine, 1991; Noguera, 2008). It would also have been difficult not to notice the students' passion for this class, which I had not observed in their other classes; hands were raised and students were squirming in their chairs for the opportunity to be heard. Latrise respectfully addressed students as "Mr." or "Ms." followed by their last names. Latrise's commitment to her students began with her own experiences sitting exactly where they sat; as she explains earlier in her story, she was a product of the same public school system and had life experiences that mirrored their own.

When it was time for Latrise's students to begin writing their poetry anthology projects, there were no moans, groans, or complaints. Latrise's students were prepared. An array of books were displayed on the dry erase marker tray to inspire students for this upcoming poetry unit, including *The Norton Anthology of Poetry*, R&B singer-actor Jill Scott's "Paint Me Like I Am," Emily Dickinson's *Final Harvest*, Walter Dean Myers's *Blues Journey*, and *Selected Poems of Langston Hughes* (see the annotated bibliography at the end of the book for summaries of these and other books we have found important for culturally relevant teaching). With the class Blackboard site beaming on the Promethean board, students journeyed through a wealth of resources including websites for poetry, additional readings, a guide to literary devices, elements of poetry, and links to audio recordings of poets reading their own work. This virtual roadmap would guide students through creating their own poetry anthology projects that had to include an introduction, analysis of poems, and synthesis of ideas.

While Latrise was not the first teacher in an urban public high school to assign this kind of writing project, it bears noting her students coveted the opportunity. Ellis High School's curriculum was moving toward being inquiry-driven; however, many ninth graders arrived from schools that focused on "urban pedagogies." Urban pedagogies, Duncan (2000) argues, focus on controlling and managing Black and Latino children as opposed to creating rigorous learning opportunities. Therefore, the work Latrise and her colleagues tried to do—give students the space to exercise agency by developing projects—was something many students never experienced in their previous years of schooling. According to Duncan (2000), "the main purpose of urban public schools in the lives of students of color has been largely to prepare them to occupy and accept subordinate roles within the U.S. economy and, by extension, society" (p. 29). It soon became clear that this poetry project defied this kind of teaching. In fact, the math, science, and social studies teachers at Ellis High School noticed students writing for their poetry anthologies throughout the day and teased Latrise about their inability to get students interested in anything else. Observing Latrise's work in this SLC, a setting that was initially a comprehensive high school failing half its children, was like watching an educational architect build a bridge over the gaps in achievement among public school students.

Our Journey

As scholars move away from the language of the "achievement gap" and argue that the disparities in American public schools are better characterized as an "educational debt" (Ladson-Billings, 2006), concerns about the differences in student achievement remain of grave importance. While the notion of culturally relevant teaching has been largely discussed in urban education circles (Irvine, 2002, 2003; Gay, 2000; Ladson-Billings, 1995), this book focuses on culturally relevant teaching in the literacy classroom, particularly in the teaching of writing. During a Leadership Policy Summit in 2005, the Conference on English Education (CEE) created a working group of English educators that focused on this very issue. Grappling with the question "What do we know and believe about supporting linguistically and culturally diverse learners in English education?" the focus group agreed that teachers needed to consider the context of their students' lives in the ways that ethnographers and anthropologists approach the communities in which they work. Arguing that "real teaching" for "real diversity" views teaching as a political act, the focus group asserted, "educators need to model culturally responsive and socially responsible practices and processes for students" (Boyd et al., 2004), which is a point we underscore throughout this book.

Notions of culturally relevant teaching arise from a strong research base that focuses on the lives and futures of diverse students. Not surprisingly, our efforts to demonstrate the role of culturally relevant teaching in the writing classroom are also undergirded by research into sound pedagogy generally. In particular, in this book we try to connect issues surrounding culturally relevant pedagogy to the *NCTE Beliefs about the Teaching of Writing*.

While all the statements connect in some ways, three in particular relate to our work:

- Everyone has the capacity to write, writing can be taught, and teachers can help students become better writers.
- Writing grows out of many different purposes.
- Literate practices are embedded in complicated social relationships.

> *Everyone has the capacity to write, writing can be taught, and teachers can help students become better writers.* Our early encounters as a literacy coach and classroom teacher in a predominantly African American school located in an economically challenged neighborhood always returned us to the belief that all of our students not only had the capacity to write but their lives depended on the ability to communicate effectively through writing. We support the notion that literacy is indeed a "civil right" and without a critical literacy education, educators are "relegating whole communities to the low-wage, military, and prison prep tracks in our society" (Lipman, 2008, p. 62). Indeed, we both have witnessed middle school teachers who never assigned writing and justified it with explanations such as "the children get too excited" and they could not get them "under control" unless they used book work or worksheets. Our challenge, and one that we welcomed, was to introduce Latrise's ninth-grade students to blank sheets of paper and writing utensils as opposed to the fill-in-the-blank worksheets they had grown accustomed to in their

elementary and middle school experiences. We both understood teachers had to be "practitioners of the craft" (Fisher, 2005a, 2005b, 2007); that is, English language arts teachers had to be readers and writers who were willing to exchange their voices and writing with their students to cultivate trust and community. We firmly believed in challenging and changing the mindset of students; they first needed to believe they had the potential to write, an idea most of them were hearing for the first time in their academic careers. In previous years, we also experienced teaching in diverse classrooms and predominantly white classrooms. Maisha's teaching experience in California taught her that all children need exposure to materials that represent alternative views and multiple experiences.

Writing grows out of many different purposes. While the aforementioned Poetry Anthology Project assigned in Latrise's class was not an expository essay or research paper, it was a way to get students excited about writing. For the purpose of this assignment, students had an opportunity to analyze poems and song lyrics as well as synthesize themes found in the collection of poetry they selected and write critiques to accompany the poems and songs themselves. Furthermore, students were invited to include forms of writing that were not traditionally included in English language arts classrooms. Many students had not imagined this kind of writing was valid or important. However, Latrise's students learned that an anthology was much more than a collection of work; it was a thoughtful mapping of work bound by a particular set of ideas or themes. We believe that students need to experience multiple writing assignments and assessments (as we talk more about in Chapter Five) in order to decide what kinds of writing will serve them best as they consider their lives beyond high school (see Chapter Three).

Literate practices are embedded in complicated social relationships. Part of creating a community of writers is providing a forum and space for young people to talk and share their ideas. Through our research and teaching experiences, we are still surprised to find that children in urban public schools are seldom given opportunities to know their opinions and ideas are important. Elsewhere, Fisher (2007) found students in urban public high schools believed they were asked to do the "school's work" that was seemingly unrelated to anything they cared about. We believe that successful teachers of students in largely failing schools and neighborhoods have established a foundation built on respect. This simple yet often taken for granted concept is embedded in important stories about teachers and their students, from Michie's (1999) experiences teaching *The House on Mango Street*, to Kinloch's (2010) students rereading gentrification in their Harlem neighborhoods as text, to Morrell's (2008) students who become ethnographers armed with the tools for analysis and synthesis, to Joe[2] reciting poetry alongside student poets in his Power Writing seminar in the Bronx (Fisher 2005a, 2005b, 2007). The teachers profiled in this book listened to their students; even if they had to revisit a lesson plan or curricular unit, they made time to infuse the needs of their students into the curriculum without sacrificing standards or high expectations. Teachers realized that to have students listen to them, they, too, had to listen and hear their students when they were trying to convey their desires in the classroom.

Journeying through This Book

The purpose of this book is to consider the ways in which culturally relevant pedagogy can be used in the English language arts classroom to motivate and inspire an emerging generation of writers. Our work as teachers, teacher educators, and researchers demonstrates the need for socially relevant pedagogical practices in order to develop and support these emerging writers in and beyond our classrooms.

In Chapter 2, "Culturally Relevant Pedagogy: The Remix," we synthesize the lessons learned from research on culturally relevant teachers and curriculum. We hope that in highlighting the salient findings, classroom teachers will feel supported in their process of becoming culturally and socially relevant in their pedagogical practices. Additionally, we hope our teacher-friendly review challenges teachers who have already implemented culturally relevant pedagogy to think about the process in new ways.

In Chapter 3, "Press Play: Culturally Relevant Pedagogy in Action," we offer pedagogical portraits of English language arts classrooms where teachers with whom we have worked grapple with ways to introduce and reintroduce culturally relevant pedagogy in their curriculum and practice. We introduce real teachers and students and examine the teaching and learning opportunities that emerged when these teachers chose to open their classroom doors to their students' world and encouraged students to connect to the experiences of others.

Once we have introduced these teachers and students, we attempt to unpack in some detail the work teachers did in their classrooms with students. In Chapter 4, "Let the Music Play: Culturally Relevant Writing Instruction," we offer ways to implement some of the strategies used by teachers we worked with as well as our own strategies for how to set the stage for writing opportunities. This chapter provides insight into resources, essential questions, and culminating projects.

In Chapter 5, "From Gold to Platinum: Assessing Student Writing," we discuss ways in which teachers can assess student writing that emerges from culturally relevant pedagogy. We offer new ways in which students may experience culturally relevant pedagogy that creates meaningful learning opportunities for them.

Finally, in an annotated bibliography we have titled "Latrise and Maisha's Infinite Playlist," we share some of our favorite resources that may or may not fall under the typical heading of culturally relevant texts; however, we offer the ways in which we have made these texts culturally and socially relevant as well as how we use them for writing instruction.

As you read, we invite you to think about your own students, your own experiences, and your own pedagogies and try to imagine how you, too, might create a culturally relevant classroom that will inspire your students' learning.

Notes

1. Southeastern Urban District and Ellis High School are pseudonyms.

2. "Joe," featured in Maisha's book *Writing in Rhythm* (2007), is a teacher who teaches a Power Writing seminar in the Bronx.

Chapter Two

Culturally Relevant Pedagogy: The Remix

The Call for Culturally Relevant Teaching in Literacy Classrooms

Before we concern ourselves with incorporating culturally relevant pedagogy into our classrooms or how writing instruction can be culturally relevant, it is important to acknowledge how and why the need for culturally relevant pedagogy arises in the first place. Due mainly to educational inequities and disparities among races, culturally relevant pedagogy was birthed out of the need to acknowledge the lives and minds of students who have been ignored and underserved in America's classrooms.

Assessment of student literacy achievement continues to reveal what has been referred to as an achievement gap between culturally diverse and white populations in school. The achievement gap refers to disparities in education among groups of students (e.g., gender, ethnicity/race, and socioeconomic status) as noted by different educational measures assessed by the National Assessment of Educational Progress (NAEP). In 2007, NAEP's assessment of reading and writing trends among students in the United States found African American, Hispanic, and Native American students scored up to 31 points lower, on average, in reading and 26 points lower, on average, in writing than their white and Asian peers (Lee, Grigg, & Donahue, 2007; Salahu-Din, Persky, & Miller, 2008). In addition to this literacy achievement gap, there is disproportionate failure among culturally diverse[1] populations in reading. Data from NAEP (2009a) reveal that only 18 percent of whites and 20 percent of Asians in the eighth grade perform at or below the basic skills level in reading, whereas 48 percent of African Americans and 44 percent of Hispanic students read below the basic skills level. The percentage of African American and Hispanic failure has not improved in almost a decade.

In contrast to the more typical depictions of the achievement gap is Ladson-Billings' (2006) concept of the *education debt*. She acknowledges the prevalence of research related to the achievement gap, yet she questions whether or not the focus on the achievement gap is indeed the best way to "explain and understand the persistent inequity that exists (and has always existed) in our nation's schools" (p. 4). Conversely, Ladson-Billings argues for a more in-depth look at historical, economic, sociopolitical, and moral debts that have led to the education deficit of African American and Latina/Latino youths who have been historically denied access to education and/or equal educational funding and are excluded from the civic process.

What's the difference between thinking of the discrepancy among students as an achievement gap versus an educational debt? If you're a teacher who accepts the explanation of the achievement gap, then you may attempt to fill your African American and Hispanic students with the knowledge that will afford them access to specific skill sets, canonical knowledge, and dominant language practices. These students may be viewed as deficient, or as missing "the stuff" needed to have life-long success. In contrast, teachers who accept the educational debt mindset may view their "marginalized" students as being owed "back-pay" as a result of historical, economic, and sociopolitical inequities endured for decades.

Whether we see it as an achievement gap, educational debt, or a nexus of the two, for years, researchers have attempted to explain academic failure, which remains at the forefront of educational reform discourse, including No Child Left Behind (NCLB). Irvine (2003) acknowledges four explanations for academic failure among marginalized youth—socioeconomic, sociopathological, genetic, and cultural—and notes the merits (excluding the genetic argument) and limitations in each. In this chapter, we briefly summarize the limitations she acknowledges in each argument. There are no simple answers to the very real problems that underscore academic failure among marginalized youth, although we believe that a move toward culturally relevant pedagogy may help us begin to counteract school failure.

The Socioeconomic Explanation

Academic failure among African Americans, Hispanics, and other minorities has been attributed to income, class, and wealth. Researchers have attempted to explain academic deficit as a result of this economic disparity. However, Irvine (2003) points out that even when African American students come from affluent families or are beneficiaries of equal per-pupil expenditures by school systems, African American students still perform significantly lower than their white counterparts. In other words, the socioeconomic argument fails to explain why upper-class and middle-class African American students still fail.

The Sociopathological Explanation

The sociopathological explanation of minority student failure considers the grim circumstances many minorities face in their homes and communities. Researchers have cited broken homes, gang violence, drugs, and poverty as reasons why minority students fail in school. Also, some researchers posit that low achievement among African American students results from "an oppositional social identity" in which academic success and intellectual activity are associated with "acting white" and, therefore, behavior undesirable for African Americans (Ogbu, 1981). However, this argument, according to Irvine (2003), "fails to acknowledge the resilience of African American people and the legacy of their preslave, African heritage. Furthermore, this position does not acknowledge how individuals' own personal experiences and their resolve to succeed act to counter society's perceptions of intellectual competence" (p. 5). Thus, the sociopathological argument to explain African American failure disregards the many African American people who have and continue to achieve not only academic success, but the prosperity that academic success has afforded them.

The Genetic Explanation

Historically, research that attempted to explain intelligence and academic achievement based on genetics used intelligence quotient (IQ) scores to suggest that African Americans are academically inferior to whites (Irvine, 2003). While most of us reject that argument outright, Irvine confronts it head on: "research literature . . . indicates that environmental factors, school attendance, and nutrition contribute to intelligence" (p. 6). In other words, the genetic argument used to explain intelligence and academic achievement has limitations in that research that uses IQ scores alone to explain intelligence does not take into account external factors that contribute to IQ scores in the first place.

The Cultural Explanation

The literature related to a cultural explanation for academic achievement does not consider the culture (e.g., language, values, norms, rituals, and symbols) of African American students as inherent problems. It does, however, suggest a cultural conflict between African American culture and the culture of school (Irvine, 2003). However, Irvine suggests that even though a cultural mismatch may exist, "the most important match is a type of seamlessness between home and school that is connected by vision, shared values, and a sense of mission and purpose" (p. 7). Thus, schools and teachers have the ability to welcome the cultural voices and perspectives of their students by allowing students' whole selves to be a part of the school practices and curriculum.

Although Irvine focuses primarily on African American youth, researchers are charting the educational experiences of Latina/Latino and Native American youth that reveal similar narratives in which culturally relevant pedagogy may or may not be part of classroom curricula (San Pedro, 2011). At best, research tells us that when culturally relevant pedagogy is included as an integral part of literacy instruction, the identities of marginalized youth are recognized and affirmed, and academic achievement is expected and possible. At worst, researchers are uncovering clues suggesting that the absence of culturally relevant pedagogy can be detrimental to the academic outcomes of students.

Remnants of classist and racist theories continue to linger in the policies and pedagogies that shape schooling for minority and poor children. Nieto (2000) suggests that "it is the school's *perception* of students' language, culture, and class as *inadequate* and *negative*, and the subsequent devalued status of these characteristics in the academic environment, that help to explain school failure" (p. 232). Nieto (2003) also attributes the lack of success in school of minority and poor children to narrow definitions of academic success and enriching activities and the propensity to uphold and confirm the experiences of the middle class as "essential to academic success."

Such that these common explanations fall short in providing real answers to a disheartening reality for African American and other minorities who continue to fail in school, there is a need to deliberately consider the education of culturally diverse students with intention and care. Educators—that is, parents, teachers, administrators, board members, teacher educators, and researchers—at all levels have a responsibility to ensure the academic success of all students. Culturally relevant pedagogy begins with the premise that all students can experience academic success, and it is our belief that educators can utilize culturally relevant pedagogy in order to ensure that marginalized populations experience academic success in our schools nationwide.

Defining and Redefining Culturally Relevant Pedagogy

Ladson-Billings (1992, 1994, 1995), Berliner (1989), Shulman (1987), Giroux and Simon (1989), and others have contributed to the definition of culturally relevant pedagogy as a critical and oppositional pedagogy that is committed to collective empowerment. In other words, culturally relevant pedagogy seeks not to merely provide knowledge as some fixed entity, but also to reconstruct knowledge in order to serve the needs of students. Culturally relevant pedagogy relies on cultural references that are relevant in the lives of students in order to impart knowledge and skills that will empower students intellectually, socially, emotionally, and politically (Ladson-Billings, 1994).

Needless to say, while culturally relevant pedagogy is beneficial in all that it does for students, it can be difficult for teachers who are not familiar with the cultures of their students. Though teachers who share cultural ties with students are more likely to incorporate shared cultural references within the classroom, culturally relevant pedagogy does not require that teachers and students share cultural identities. It does, however, require that teachers become "culturally immersed" in their students' cultures to facilitate effective teaching and learning (Karunuñgan, 2002). Becoming "culturally immersed" does not require that teachers embark on some distant journey into the cultural abyss of each of their students. They are certain to get lost. It does, however, command a certain disposition—one that can regard students as experts, one that is open to learning about the lives of students, and one that can push students to connect their lives to the world around them.

We think it is important to address and make clear that culturally relevant pedagogy is not just for students of color. It is not just incorporating African American authors or stories about Hispanics. Neither is it a survey of genres authored by people at the margins. Certainly, many would argue that culturally relevant pedagogy requires that you invite the powerful voices of those who are generally overlooked in the texts and curriculum of American education; and that is undoubtedly an important aspect. However, culturally relevant pedagogy is also about the students who show up in our classrooms daily. It welcomes students' voices, demands their reflection, and pushes them toward discovery of self. Culturally relevant pedagogy validates students' existence regardless of class, race, ethnicity, economic status, or academic level.

Culturally Relevant Pedagogy

Culturally relevant pedagogy humanizes, respects, and considers the histories, perspectives, and experiences of students as an essential part of the subject matter, classroom practices, and content of educative practices and spaces. It considers students' experiences as legitimate and official content for the class curriculum.

The bottom line is teachers want ways to help their students achieve inside and outside of their classrooms. It is not enough to simply adopt culturally relevant pedagogy without understanding that there are outcomes to culturally relevant pedagogy that provide tangible benefits for students. Ladson-Billings (1995) outlines three criteria in which culturally relevant pedagogy rests: (a) students must experience academic success, (b) students must develop and/or maintain cultural competence, and (c) students must develop a critical consciousness (sociopolitical consciousness) through which they challenge the status quo of the current social order. The following is a brief description of each criterion. We will illustrate how such criteria play out in terms of writing instruction in culturally relevant classrooms in Chapters 3 and 4.

Academic Success

Ladson-Billings (1995) maintains that despite the current social and hostile classroom environments that may exist, students must develop their literacy, numeracy, technological, social, and political skills to be active participants in society. Culturally relevant pedagogy seeks not only to empower students in order to combat what may be socially hostile environments, it also provides students with the opportunities to build upon their academic competencies as well as achieve academic success. The benefit for students is that they not only achieve academic success, but that they have reason to embrace knowledge and buy into a process that we have made them a part of. In other words, because culturally relevant pedagogy acknowledges their voices and perspectives as an integral part of what they will learn, students invoke an important principle: that education is important, that education is a part of them, and that they are a part of education.

Cultural Competence

Culturally relevant pedagogy requires that students maintain cultural integrity as well as academic success (Ladson-Billings, 1995). In a culturally relevant classroom, students' culture is an integral part of the educative practices. In other words, what students know and understand about themselves is welcomed as a part of the curriculum, discussions, and class activities. Therefore, students are able to maintain their cultural connections while at the same time gaining the skills that are required for academic success. In this way, students feel empowered. Learning is accessible and no longer an isolated occurrence that happens for some and not others. Because culturally relevant pedagogy uses the cultural competencies of students, learning happens as a result of, rather than in spite of, their presence.

Critical Consciousness

In addition to promoting academic success and cultural consciousness, culturally relevant pedagogy invites students to develop a broader sociopolitical consciousness that provides space for them to critique cultural norms, values, mores, and institutions that produce and maintain social inequities (Ladson-Billings, 1992). This means that culturally relevant spaces and practices encourage students to evaluate the world in which they live. When students are provided the opportunity to critique the world around them in the classroom, they practice the life skill of analyzing and assessing how their ideologies are similar to or different from those that shape society. They gain a skill that allows them to continually challenge stereotypes, push boundaries, and reshape ideologies that perpetuate the status quo.

Literacy and the Call for Culturally Relevant Teaching

Research continues to present a mismatch between the "literate currency" (Obidah, 1998) of minority students and the literacy expectations of teachers who dominate English and language arts classrooms. Scholars suggest a number of reasons for this so-called mismatch that often leads to student indifference, alienation, and/or student failure, including teachers' low expectations for students (Irvine, 1992), teachers' misinterpretation of student needs and backgrounds (Siddle-Walker, 1992), and teachers' unawareness of what is meaningful in the everyday lives of their students (Delpit, 1996). Culturally relevant pedagogy calls for a broad conception of literacy that incorporates literature and oratory skills (Ladson-Billings, 1992). A broader definition, or ideological view of literacy, allows for the incorporation of the reading, writing, speaking, and performance practices that are customary in the lives of youth.

In today's literacy classrooms, the reading, writing, and speaking that students are expected to do often do not reflect practical approaches to teaching literacy that are culturally relevant. In other words, culturally relevant teaching without the consideration of its practical application to the teaching and learning of literacy just becomes one more isolated part of the curriculum. Ladson-Billings (1992) presents practical approaches to teaching literacy as the following:

1. *Literacy instruction should validate students' cultures by casting all texts initially from their cultural frame of reference.* In other words, students should experience texts that affirm their identities and support their cultural knowledge.

2. *Literacy instruction should deal explicitly with race and culture.* Classroom texts, discussions, and activities should be provided which invite students to deal with race and culture up front.

3. *Literacy instruction should include Standard English to speak and teach, but also should invite other forms of English (e.g., African American Vernacular English*

[AAVE] and Spanglish) in informal situations and allow students' home language to be spoken in the classroom. At the same time, teachers should help students learn to switch between Standard English and other forms of English.

Examples of how several teachers use culturally relevant approaches in their literacy instruction will be highlighted in a series of vignettes in Chapter 3.

The New Playlist: Contemporary Voices Speak Culturally Relevant Pedagogy

Many researchers, scholars, administrators, and teachers continue to look for ways to foster relationships between curriculum and the lives of young people. Scholars have conducted studies and observed educative spaces that utilize pedagogic strategies that are culturally relevant in that they consider the identities, perspectives, histories, and experiential knowledge of youth; provide space in which students are encouraged to question the world around them; and foster academic success. In his work with urban youth, Ernest Morrell (2008), for example, employs culturally relevant pedagogy through the lens of popular culture to bridge students' out-of-school literacies (that is, the literate practices that are a part of students' homes, communities, and participation in/with popular culture and media) to the literacies needed for academic success. Morrell designed and implemented a yearlong unit in his high school English classroom in which he bridged popular culture texts and canonical texts in order to develop and maintain students' academic and literate competencies. In one unit, for example, students compared a classic poem with a hip-hop song; the students read, discussed, and wrote about T. S. Eliot's "Love Song of J. Alfred Prufrock" and Grand Master Flash's "The Message" (p. 99). Morrell considered hip-hop's relevance to and influence on his students' lives and used their knowledge and experience with hip-hop to develop their academic literacies.

Scholars also have documented instances in which educators use the literate identities of youth to create culturally relevant teaching and learning opportunities that foster academic success for all students. Educators create opportunities in language arts classrooms in which the knowledge, histories, and perspectives of students are not only considered, but also validated. Such researchers and educators assent to expanded notions of literacy and culturally relevant teaching which, along with reading, writing, and speaking, include literacies and skills that students use daily as they encounter personal, social, and highly technical mediums. Mahiri (2004) explores the use of African American youth culture as a bridge to writing development through his students' writing of "street scripts." Here the writings of the students are used as a lens through which they are able to reflect on their lives as well as critique their world in the way that they understand it. Hill (2009) provides an examination of the role of hip-hop texts and how students use them "to negotiate particular conceptions of self and the social world" (p. 5). Hill developed a Hip-Hop Lit course in which students engaged hip-hop texts in ways they would engage more traditional texts (e.g., written analysis, discussion, response writing, composing). Kirkland (2007) explores the possibility of using hip-hop as text in order for students to engage in critical thinking, textual analysis, discussion, and writing, all skills important to any English language arts classroom. Lee (2000) explores a similar approach by using students' knowledge of signifying and rap music to teach literary interpretation. In an ethnography conducted in a high school in New York City, Fisher (2005a, 2005b, 2007) examines a writing program in which students participate in "power writing" as they examine their own lives to find inspiration for original poetry.

By expanding the definition of literacy to include the literate practices of youth who are traditionally marginalized, we invoke principles of culturally relevant pedagogy. In more recent work, Kirkland (2009) explores the literate identity of a young African American man who uses "texts and tattoos to revise a shattered self portrait" (p. 376). In his essay, Kirkland examines how Derrick's tattoos represent a part of his literate identity in which his body serves as the space where he shares stories, copes with tragedy, and philosophizes. As culturally relevant pedagogy considers the lived experiences of students, an expanded notion of literacy then invites students' experiences with all types of texts. A lot of this work has been considered in out-of-school spaces, but we believe it provides the basis for work that might transfer to in-school contexts. Kinloch (2010), for example, explores the possibilities posed by the intersection of literacy and place in the lives of youth in a case study in which Phillip, a young African American male high school student, documents (using multiple media) his thoughts on the gentrification of Harlem. Using several approaches to his storytelling, Phillip engages in writing, speaking, performing, analyzing, and critiquing—acts of literacy engagement that are valuable to language arts classrooms. Educators and researchers continue to investigate ways in which expanded notions of literacy and culturally relevant pedagogy invite the voices and perspectives of students as well as connect with their ever-changing literate lives.

From each scholar, we gain valuable understandings of the possibilities of utilizing culturally relevant pedagogy in English and language arts classrooms. Below, we provide a bulleted list of what we can learn from these scholars in order to inform our own culturally relevant teaching:

• Teachers should consider students' out-of-school literacies as a way to connect their perspectives, experiences, and knowledge to what they learn in English and language arts classrooms (Morrell, 2008).

- Popular culture can serve as curriculum in which students examine it along with more traditional texts to develop and maintain their literate competencies (Morrell, 2008).

- Hip-hop, song lyrics, magazine articles, blogs, and editorials can serve as text in which students can examine literary structure, discuss relevant political and social issues, understand the influences of "poets" through both historical and contemporary lenses (Morrell, 2008; Hill, 2009), and engage critical thinking and textual analysis (Lee, 2000; Kirkland, 2007).

- A broad view of literacy can allow for the inclusion of literate practices that welcome the voices and perspectives of youth (Fisher, 2007; Kirkland, 2009).

A Template for Culturally Relevant Pedagogy

Culturally relevant pedagogy includes the methods and practices of teaching that connect students (i.e., their experiential knowledge, backgrounds, perspectives) to curriculum in order to yield positive academic, cultural, and social outcomes. Culturally relevant pedagogy requires specific behaviors on the parts of teachers and students. Also, certain aspects of space have to be considered in which culturally relevant practices that take place are integral to the teaching and learning that happens in a classroom from day to day.

Based on the work of the scholars mentioned earlier and others, we have constructed a template that describes some conditions under which culturally relevant teaching and learning can occur. We believe that teachers, practices, curriculum, and space can coexist to create culturally relevant experiences that will lead students to achieve academic success, maintain cultural competence, and develop a critical consciousness. Behaviors and actions by teachers and students and characteristics of the curriculum and physical space encourage positive student outcomes and can foster academic success for students. The following lists contain criteria for a culturally relevant praxis.

Culturally Relevant Teachers

The phrase "culturally relevant teachers" is used to describe those who consider culturally relevant pedagogy and content as a part of the daily curriculum. Culturally relevant teachers use students' perspectives, backgrounds, and experiential knowledge when planning and delivering content in order to encourage student academic development. The following tenets describe central behaviors of teachers that enable the permeation of culturally relevant pedagogy. Culturally relevant teachers:

- Are concerned about and aware of racial and socioeconomic inequities
- Have high expectations for all students

- Acknowledge their own culture
- Are aware that who they are individually and culturally has an impact on teaching
- Are enthusiastic, passionate, and knowledgeable about their subject matter

Culturally Relevant Spaces

The phrase "culturally relevant spaces" is used to describe the physical and meta-physical aspects of educative spaces (in and out of school) that are structured in a way that is welcoming to the identities of students. Culturally relevant spaces comprise print material and text that are reflective of the lives and identities of the students who occupy such space. Culturally relevant spaces also encompass policies, ideals, and strategies that are democratic and equal. The following tenets describe how educative spaces can encourage culturally relevant teaching to take place. Culturally relevant spaces:

- Are recognized as a microcosm of larger society
- Validate students' identities
- Reflect a democratic society
- Welcome diversity
- Seek to dismantle instances of inequity

Culturally Relevant Practices

The phrase "culturally relevant practices" is used to refer to the day-to-day instances of teaching and learning that take place in educative spaces. Culturally relevant practices empower students as full participants in their own learning. The following tenets describe culturally relevant class operations, pedagogical strate-gies, and teacher praxis, which can foster academic success for students. Culturally relevant practices:

- Demonstrate fluidity in teacher and student relationships
- Show knowledge as being continually re-created and shared by students and teachers
- Share student and teacher experiential knowledge
- Empower students to exercise agency in how and what they learn
- Provide opportunity to question, research, and evaluate

Culturally Relevant Curriculum

The phrase "culturally relevant curriculum" refers to content that recognizes the knowledge, histories, and perspectives of students. It is important to note that culturally relevant curriculum may or may not be a part of the standard curriculum. For example, the Common Core Curriculum Initiative—a set of curricular standards adopted by 43 of 50 states—does not mention culturally relevant curriculum specifically. However, culturally relevant curriculum can supplement, complement, and/or contradict state and national curricula. The following tenets describe qualities of culturally relevant curriculum that provide the basis on which culturally relevant praxis can happen. Culturally relevant curriculum:

- Is liberating
- Is not dependent on state or national curriculum
- Is inquiry-driven
- Legitimizes the lived-experiences of students
- Challenges all students regardless of perceived abilities or cultural limitations

Student Outcomes as a Result of Culturally Relevant Teachers, Spaces, Practices, and Curriculum

If teachers are the *who*, spaces are the *where*, practices are the *what*, and curriculum is the *how*, then the students are the *why*. Culturally relevant pedagogy can promote the academic success of all students. If you as a teacher situate your teaching within the tenets of culturally relevant pedagogy, your students can learn to engage the world critically, recognize learning as a way to give back to the community, and make connections between their communities, the nation, and the world. If you are wondering about the *when*, culturally relevant teaching can take place at any time, for any content, by any teacher.

Writing That Is Culturally Relevant

Writing is increasingly important to a world that is becoming more textual with each passing day. We and our students encounter countless instances in which we must engage in some kind of text. Before even entering the school building, students encounter text on their cell phones, social networking sites (e.g., Facebook, MySpace, Twitter, Bebo, World of Warcraft), advertisements, billboards, magazines, as well as their own personal writing.

Current research on writing instruction seeks to examine novel ways to teach and assess student writing. Researchers use several terms to describe the kinds of writing that should take place in current classroom communities, including authentic (Khan, 2009), innovative (Kinloch, 2009a), real-world (Cox et al., 2009), process-driven (Fisher, Purcell, & May, 2009), and purposeful. These terms are related in the sense that they provide opportunities for students to use their own experiential knowledge and apply it to writing activities in the classroom. Culturally relevant writing, though closely related to the aforementioned writing in which the "lives and experiences [of students] naturally bring interesting information, concrete details, observation, and description, and narrative lines to a writing piece" (Moore-Hart, 2005, p. 328), seeks to allow students to examine and question sociocultural and sociopolitical realities that affect their lives. In other words, culturally relevant writing permits young people to reflect on issues and interrogate them while employing multiple literacies. Culturally relevant writing makes students more capable writers in that they have the opportunity to recognize and write for authentic audiences and purposes that matter to them.

Culturally Relevant Writing Pedagogy

Culturally relevant writing pedagogy invites the voices of students and creates a space for them to take on issues that reflect their cultural, social, and personal experiences. It humanizes, respects, and considers the histories, perspectives, and experiences of students as an essential part of the subject matter, classroom practices, and content of educative practices and spaces while considering content, organization, audience, tone, vocabulary, and other elements of writing. Culturally relevant writing pedagogy legitimizes students' voices, knowledge, and experiences as official content of the class curriculum.

Out of culturally relevant practice comes an expanded notion of literacy in which the voices, perspectives, and lived experiences of students are considered. The aforementioned research provides a template for culturally relevant writing in which students engage in writing that "[links] the day's topic to their own ideas and experiences" (Hill, 2009, p. 24), "[revises] a shattered self-portrait" (Kirkland, 2009, p. 375), reimagines community "from just simply a 'place to sleep'" (Kinloch, 2009a, p. 333), and "examines their 'multiple identities' and 'hyphenated selves'" (Fisher, Purcell, & May, 2009, p. 338).

What does a culturally relevant writing approach look like in an actual classroom? The following chapter explores pedagogical portraits of how some actual teachers have employed culturally relevant writing, as well as illustrates what we consider benefits to implementing culturally relevant pedagogy in general, and culturally relevant writing specifically, in language arts classrooms.

Note

1. *Culturally diverse* is used here to describe populations that are nonwhite or populations that assume customs, traditions, languages, sexual orientations, values, etc., that deviate from those that are deemed "normal" (i.e., white, heterosexual, middle class).

Chapter Three

Press Play: Culturally Relevant Pedagogy in Action

Ms. Jane and Mrs. Flowers,[1] the tenth- and ninth-grade English language arts teachers at the Ellis Small Learning Community, or SLC, enjoyed being neighbors: their classrooms shared a wall and they exchanged resources, ideas, and sources of inspiration. And like many neighbors, they were very different—in both teaching style and personality, differences that contributed to the diverse teaching community that existed at Ellis.

Ms. Jane jumped into students' conversations, laughed easily at their jokes, and proudly demonstrated her ease with the popular culture students embraced. She moved around the classroom rapidly, always leaving students guessing as to where she would appear next. Ms. Jane's unpredictability kept students on their toes and they looked forward to her class. Desks were organized in a large rectangle where everyone could see each other, with a small opening where the Promethean board clung to the wall.

Mrs. Flowers, in contrast, embodied elegance and grace. Her students spoke in a low volume that she modeled as she gracefully moved around the room. While Mrs. Flowers relied on nonverbal cues to inform students when they needed to focus, she had a quiet way of appealing to students' sense of personal best. Students' desks were permanently organized in cooperative groups of four. The girls in particular adored her, especially after she created and advised an after school program focused on cultivating girls' leadership skills, a welcomed addition to a largely male school.

Despite these differences in style, management, and personality between the two teachers, the camaraderie and rapport Ms. Jane and Mrs. Flowers had with each other created a welcoming space for students and for student teachers placed in their classrooms.

In this chapter, we provide pedagogical portraits of these two teachers' classrooms and the classrooms of two student teachers, Ms. Luz and Ms. Iman, in order to demonstrate both how these teachers integrated a culturally relevant pedagogy into their classrooms and how they synthesized their ideas, philosophies, and understandings of the role of culturally relevant pedagogy with writing instruction. What we're calling here a pedagogical portrait is the intersection of several teachers' educational philosophies, self-reflections, and actual practices. As researchers in the classrooms in this school, we were able to observe these teachers and talk to them about their practices, wearing one of our hats—that of an ethnographer. In that role and through these teachers' stories, we aim to show—as opposed to tell—what takes place in English language arts classrooms, where teachers are grappling with teaching writing and forging meaningful connections with students' lives. We invite these teachers to speak for themselves through the words we gathered from qualitative interviews with them, interviews that invoke the kind of reflection that all of us must engage in and sustain throughout our careers as educators. We begin the chapter by offering some background context for Ellis SLC. And in the last pages, we ask (and respond to) "What do these pedagogical portraits tell us?" as we prepare for an expanded look in Chapter 4 at successful practices and strategies for teaching culturally relevant writing—that is, in this chapter, we will identify the salient characteristics of the curriculum in these classrooms and then offer in the next chapter ways to use this curriculum to incite and inspire writing in our classrooms.

Ellis SLC: A Space Ready for Culturally Relevant Pedagogy

To understand the work of Ms. Jane, Mrs. Flowers, and their two student teachers, Ms. Luz and Ms. Iman, it is essential to know that Ellis SLC was one part of the first large comprehensive high school in its district to transition into four small learning communities (SLCs). Important to note in this context is that the large comprehensive high school that preceded the small learning communities served mostly African American students from underserved communities and in its old capacity graduated less than half of its students. As part of a new initiative, the school was closed and then reopened as four small learning communities. Each SLC had its own theme, principal, staff that began with approximately five teachers, and 100 ninth graders. Each year a new grade 9 cohort of approximately 100 students was added to each SLC so that there would never be more than 400 students total per SLC. Each SLC made use of advisory classes, providing opportunities for teachers to work with a small number of students throughout their high school experience and engage in topics and issues that were not always a part of the regular curriculum (see Poliner & Lieber, 2004). The use of advisory groups, sometimes referred to as "family groups," has been on the rise in urban classrooms, often as a space to engage students in writing experiences extending beyond the typical English language arts curriculum (Fisher 2005a, 2005b, 2007; Winn & Ubiles, 2011). Ellis focused on grade-level team planning as opposed to department meetings organized by disciplines. Therefore, the English teachers seldom had opportunities to work together with the exception of a monthly campus-wide meeting with English teachers from the other SLCs. While many teachers shared the same ethnic identity—African American—as Ellis students, they were still living in different worlds with regards to socioeconomic status as well as cultural interests, such as music (the rapper T. I. was hailed by the students as the "king"), clothing style (teachers enjoyed their role as the fashion police, reminding boys to "pull up your pants" and girls to "dress like ladies"), hair styles (mohawks and dreadlocks were in abundance in addition to surprising streaks of hot pink, red, and occasional blue that could be found in an otherwise plain ponytail), and speech (teachers frequently asked students to translate their newly invented words).

SLCs have become, among other things, a response to the so-called achievement gap or "educational debt," as discussed in Chapter 2. However, it should also be noted that small is not enough (Ancess, 2008); SLCs still need an intellectually rigorous curriculum and a staff committed to creating a safety net for all youth. The focus of the particular SLC at Ellis was to prepare students for college level work through an inquiry-driven curriculum that underscored literacy—especially writing—in all content areas. This was a lofty aim and one that we both, in different capacities, worked to make happen. Latrise was on the initial team of teachers who opened the school, designed curriculum, and developed a schoolwide writing culture; and Maisha was the school "coach" who worked with all teachers to integrate literacy into their pedagogical practices through co-planning, co-teaching, and facilitating learning opportunities (faculty forums) for teachers. Over the four years we worked in the school, Latrise began her graduate program but continued to serve as a mentor and supervisor to student teachers in English language arts classes at Ellis. Maisha continued her work as a coach at Ellis until the school celebrated its first graduating class—a ceremony we both attended with immense humility and respect.

During our work with Ellis teachers, we kept returning to some enduring questions about the role of culturally relevant pedagogy in writing instruction. These questions emerged from our work as teachers and with teachers as well as from our work as researchers compelled by the intersections of race, class, gender, and notions of critical literacy. Some of our guiding questions included these:

- What is culturally relevant pedagogy in the context of the English language arts classroom?

- In what ways does culturally relevant pedagogy help inspire and facilitate the writing process?

- How can teachers use culturally relevant pedagogy to help students chart a path from their local selves (thinking about themselves, their families, communities) to their global selves (considering the ways in which their lives are linked to the lives of others)? How does this kind of pedagogy support writing?

While these questions continue to guide our work, we are also keenly interested in the incredible opportunities that English teachers have more generally to create literacy communities that honor the young people before them. In an English classroom, students can be introduced to literature, poetry, plays, music, as well as nonwritten texts and, in the best cases, be transformed in positive ways by the experience. For some children in urban public schools, the option to read about someone who is like them or write about themselves has not always been available. We are still amazed during our work at schools at how many students do not have opportunities to introduce themselves through writing, build empathy through literature, or simply be asked what kinds of writing and reading they are doing beyond the school walls.

Our own research demonstrates how literacy instruction can create strong communities and increased opportunities for learning. Latrise, for example, has developed case studies of middle school boys that revealed how the boys regarded their literate practices as everything from reading football and basketball plays to writing music to preparing to pray (Johnson, 2010). Taking time to sit and ask these eighth graders what they were doing in and out of school opened a door between home and school. In Maisha's work with student poets and their teachers in an urban public high school in the Bronx, she learned that students were journaling and writing poetry, raps, and song lyrics long before they entered their English language arts classrooms and yet sometimes there was no evidence in these classrooms that students could even write. It was not until one teacher, "Poppa Joe," invited students' voices, ideas, and original poetry and prose to his classroom that the school realized the potential of this diverse community of students. Elsewhere, Maisha's work with a woman-focused theater company that teaches playwriting and theater techniques to incarcerated and formerly incarcerated girls examines how playwriting, and the performance of these plays, helped teen girls engage their peers, families, and teachers, as the scripts served as a way to enter a dialogue about issues that disrupted their educational process (Winn, 2011; Winn, 2010a, 2010b).

In all of these cases, students explored their shifting identities through their work. Here is where we see culturally relevant pedagogy entering the conversation. Culturally relevant pedagogy is not merely an invitation for students to explore their lived experiences, ideas, and communities, but it can provide ways to map these individual experiences onto a global platform. However, students and teachers cannot stop there; once students have opportunities to explore their rich heritage and contributions to the "literate and literary" (McHenry & Heath, 1994; Fisher, 2004), they must learn about new people, places, and ideas. In this mapping, students learn they are not the only ones who are experiencing particular life events and they thus become open to the lives and experiences of others. Writing classrooms can and must be a site for this kind of "literocracy" in which literacy and democratic engagement form a dialectical relationship with literature, multiple texts, and genres of writing to help students think about student worlds and beyond (Fisher, 2005a, 2005b).

In the pedagogical portraits that follow, you'll have a chance to see Ms. Jane, Mrs. Flowers, and Ms. Luz and Ms. Iman at work, integrating culturally relevant pedagogy into their writing instruction. As you read, you might consider how their stances toward teaching, toward students, and toward literacy take shape in the curriculum they offer and lead them to new insights about culturally relevant teaching.

Pedagogical Portrait #1: "They brought the now to me": Social and Political Relevance in Persuasive Writing

While Ms. Jane entered Ellis with some knowledge of culturally relevant teaching from her teacher preparation and master's programs, it was her students who helped her understand the role of culturally relevant pedagogy in the writing classroom:

> Culturally relevant teaching validates writing. Watching the kids' openness to the reading when they see a name that looks like theirs or if it's a name they are familiar with makes them willing to listen at that point. . . . [E]ven the most reluctant student wants to put their mark in the conversation in some relevant way. I may not get a five-paragraph essay from them but they are building confidence when they see an intellectual discussion building from something they said in class or on Discussion Board [an electronic discussion that is part of the course Blackboard website] which will eventually lead to writing.

Ms. Jane entered the teaching profession as a substitute teacher in 1997 and was later hired in a permanent position at an ethnically diverse public high school in an urban southeastern city. While her former high school boasted an ethnically and economically diverse student body, Ms. Jane noted most of the classrooms were segregated and tracked. Additionally, most African American students at her previous school had very different experiences from their white peers—many walked to school from nearby housing projects while the majority of the white students lived in the cloistered upper-middle-class neighborhood surrounding the school. When Ms. Jane came to Ellis, she welcomed the opportunity to teach in an SLC, believing there would be a "family environment" where she could build relationships with students and create a forum in her classroom to begin the writing process.

Hoping to use culturally relevant teaching as a scaffold to writing, Ms. Jane believed that the most salient characteristic of this pedagogical strategy was "building confidence" in emerging writers, a theme that emerged throughout the teachers' classrooms we studied for the purpose of this book. One particular moment in the class demonstrates this. Ms. Jane had completed the finishing touches on a persuasive writing unit and was set to begin teaching when a discussion in her tenth-grade advisory class forced her to reconsider the way she approached the unit. One of her students, a 16-year-old African American boy named Tony, was visibly shaken by his brother's recent experience of being assaulted by police officers in their neighborhood. Ms. Jane realized that Tony and all of her students were distracted by this recent event. Students were also angry about the recurring issue of what they saw more generally as police harassment and brutality in their neighborhoods. Since Ms. Jane taught all of the tenth graders at Ellis, she considered drawing from her students' emotion and passion about police brutality to fuel their writing:

> The [police brutality] conversation resonated. Students [were] encountering this all around. We started our first "word of the day" which was "disenfranchised." And [we discussed] what happens when a person is disenfranchised as well as what [are the things] people do to make someone feel disenfranchised or like they're not a citizen.

One of Ms. Jane's struggles throughout the semester had been to convince students that their writing could create or incite change. Every day students were bearing witness to injustice and discrimination, yet they lacked access to forums where they could write about what they were seeing, hearing, and living. Ms. Jane began to consider how the persuasive genre, one of the performance standards for tenth graders both in her school district and throughout the state, could result in a writing assignment for students to grapple with tensions in their community as well as nationally surrounding police brutality and increasing surveillance in their schools. This practice echoes *NCTE Beliefs about the Teaching of Writing*, specifically that writing "grows out of many different purposes." As she incorporated this approach, Ms. Jane demonstrated that, even in a standards and test-driven climate, it was not only possible but necessary to find authentic writing tasks that motivated her students.

At the beginning of the semester, Ms. Jane could see how much her students enjoyed discussing current events and various topics. She knew that her students were fluid with language during whole-group instruction, an idea that resonated with the work of Lisa Delpit (1996). During these discussions students did not worry about rules and conventions but spoke with great passion and prior knowledge. However, Ms. Jane did not see the same fluidity she heard during discussions reflected in her students' writing. Ms. Jane wanted to move students from the rich and lively oral discussions they were already having to using writing as a tool to support their positions and explore multiple perspectives. She consistently reminded students that they already possessed a wealth of material to write about, as they discussed potential writing assignments daily. Calling on the emotion Tony and his peers had shown, she adapted the persuasive writing assignment she had been working on to reflect their passion. The revised assignment began by asking students to read an opening piece about police brutality, write a reflection on the article, and post their initial ideas on police brutality using the Discussion Board tool on the course Blackboard website. These posts could be open-ended and were designed for the students to raise questions and challenge assumptions. While Discussion Board posts can be set to "anonymous" by teachers or whoever manages the site, most of Ms. Jane's students owned their words and ideas, in part, perhaps, because she was so accepting and encouraging of their ideas. An additional way in which the posts helped students transition from speaking to writing was their conversational nature; students could write without worrying about being graded on mechanics. Discussion Board also allows teachers to track students' views individually and collectively.

The opening reading Ms. Jane used to prepare students for the Discussion Board exercise was an article on a recent police brutality case in Oakland, California. Oscar Grant, a young African American man and father of a young child, was shot and killed by one of the Bay Area Rapid Transit (BART) officers in the early hours of New Years Day 2009. Mr. Grant had already submitted to the officers' command to get on the ground and was shot and killed in spite of the fact he was unarmed and did not resist their commands. Ellis students along with the entire nation saw the disturbing video footage showing Grant being shot and killed on the nightly news.

Using current events, especially those that have the potential to reflect the lives and experiences of students, as a way to inspire students to use their pens and paper as tools for social change has long been a pedagogical tool for teachers who

are committed to culturally relevant pedagogy. One striking example was the work
of Mama C—a teacher and literacy coach in a small learning community in Brook-
lyn serving predominately African American students—who helped her students
transform their anguish over the murder of an unarmed peer, Timothy Stansbury,
by a public housing security guard into writing that was shared at forums, ral-
lies, and on radio programs (Fisher, 2008, 2009). Similarly, Ms. Jane's students
used their writing as a way to challenge some of the frustrations they and others
felt around issues with law enforcement. Expanding from that initial introduction to the specific case of Oscar Grant, students next read a controversial article
entitled "America's Police Brutality Pandemic"[2] in which the author, Paul Craig
Roberts, compared police brutality to acts of terrorism. Ms. Jane purposefully used
a provocative piece of writing to get students started. She then asked students to
begin their writing process using the Discussion Board. One of Ms. Jane's students,
Sonia, initiated a dialogue while her classmates, Les and Sonny, contributed:

> **Sonia:** [The police] are [here] to protect us. As it happens with most
> people who are handed power, the police men begin to take
> advantage and to think too much of themselves. Soon, they
> become as Roberts described them: "The only terrorist most
> Americans will ever encounter is a policeman with a badge,
> nightstick, mace and Taser."

> **Les:** I also agree with Sonia. The police are the ones who are sup-
> pose to protect the people. The police force are the ones abus-
> ing their power and taking advantage of innocent people. How
> can anyone trust the police? Honestly I feel it's very sad that the
> people we as a nation look up [to] are those who are killing.

> **Sonny:** Sonia was right. She and I both seem to agree with the response
> given by Mr. Roberts because people want to live life and not
> live in fear of the police because they have the upperhand; they
> don't run the country.

As students found ways to engage each other around Roberts's article, Sonia set the
tone and earned the respect of her peers who agreed with her perspective. Sonia,
Les, Sonny, and others used their writing to raise questions about whether or not
police officers should be held to different standards than so-called civilians. Additional Discussion Board postings also demonstrated students' desire to trust police
officers rather than fear them. What became clear through these written dialogues
was that the article provided students with a foundation to raise critical questions
about the role of law enforcement in urban communities. Discussion Board pro-

vided a live forum to complement some of the lively oral discussions, but this time in writing.

In Ms. Jane's view, culturally relevant pedagogy in the writing classroom included social and political relevance:

> [Changing my persuasive unit] literally started with a conversation in Advisory that leaked into third period where one of my students' brothers was a victim of police brutality. [The incident] had their attention. In that conversation we discussed disenfranchisement because we just finished working on a Sojourner Truth project. Our next project was working on disenfranchisement and the power of persuasion. Police brutality was on the top of their hearts. Many students knew their classmate's brother. Students were saying, "That happened to me. I knew it was not right but I did not know it was illegal." I looked over my plans to see what part of this worked with my [persuasive writing] unit. At the time I was trying to see how I was going to make the connection to disenfranchisement. I was trying to see how to make the topic fit into right now but *they brought the right now to me*. It was just one of those moments. If they were hot about this topic then let's keep the fire.

What are the implications for teachers being open to students bringing "the right now" to the classroom? Several literacy researchers that we mentioned in Chapter 2 are exploring "the right now" in youth culture and how it contributes to our understanding of the teaching and learning of literacy. Some of the "right now" is evidenced in the studies of language in the classrooms (Gutiérrez & Vossoughi, 2010), spoken word poetry in the lives of urban youth (Jocson, 2008; Fisher, 2005b, 2007), and use of hip-hop in the language arts classroom (Hill, 2009; Morrell, 2008). Like the teachers and scholars in these articles, Ms. Jane used students' prior knowledge to inform her teaching. By creating a space for students to bring "the right now" to her, Ms. Jane demonstrated how listening, talking, and exchanging ideas were important to the writing process. Additionally, Ms. Jane struck a balance between standardized curriculum and student interest; persuasive writing is a part of the performance standard both in her district and across many states. And while the study of Ms. Jane's classroom preceded the Common Core State Standards being adopted in the state where she taught, it is important to note the Common Core State Standards' delineation between persuasive writing and argument: "When writing to persuade, writers employ a variety of persuasive strategies. . . . The Standards place special emphasis on writing logical arguments as a particularly important form of college- and career-ready writing" (Common Core State Standards, Appendix A, p. 24). Argument is also included in the Common Core State Standards for writing in English language arts and literacy in history/social studies, science, and technical subjects. Other states, as well, emphasize persuasive writing as important.

Georgia Performance Standards for Tenth-Grade Literature and Composition
(retrieved from https://www.georgiastandards.org/Standards/Georgia%20Performance%20
Standards/Grade-Ten-with-asks.pdf)

All modes or genres are practiced at each grade level; however, in order to achieve mastery each grade level has a particular writing focus. Persuasive writing is the focus for 10th grade; by the end of 10th grade, the student will demonstrate competency in persuasive writing. The student writes coherent and focused texts that convey a well-defined perspective or tightly-reasoned argument. The writing exhibits the student's awareness of audience and purpose. When appropriate, the texts contain introductions, supporting evidence, and conclusions. The student regularly progresses through the stages of the writing process (e.g., prewriting, drafting, revising, and editing successive versions).

California Performance Standards for Ninth- and Tenth-Grade Writing
(retrieved from http://www.cde.ca.gov/be/st/ss/documents/elacontentstnds.pdf)

Write persuasive compositions:

    a. Structure ideas and arguments in a sustained and logical fashion.

    b. Use specific rhetorical devices to support assertions (e.g., appeal to logic through reasoning; appeal to emotion or ethical belief; relate a personal anecdote, case study, or analogy).

    c. Clarify and defend positions with precise and relevant evidence, including facts, expert opinions, quotations, and expressions of commonly accepted beliefs and logical reasoning.

    d. Address readers' concerns, counterclaims, biases, and expectations.

New York City Performance Standards
(retrieved from http://schools.nyc.gov/offices/teachlearn/documents/standards/ELA/hs/157 overview.html)

The high school standards are set at a level of performance approximately equivalent to the end of tenth grade. It is expected that some students might achieve this level earlier and others later than this grade.

Writing:

    a) Produce a report of information.

    b) Produce a response to literature.

    c) Produce a narrative account (fictional or autobiographical).

    d) Produce a narrative procedure.

    e) Produce a persuasive essay.

    f) Produce a reflective essay.

Often teachers are concerned that inviting students to write about themselves or issues close to home is somehow separate and distinct from the kind of teaching that will help them become successfully literate students. However, in *Reading, Writing, and Rising Up*, Christensen (2000) argues, "Bringing student issues into the [class]room does not mean giving up teaching the core ideas and skills of the class; it means using the energy of their connections to drive us through the content" (p. 5). Some studies have demonstrated how student writing in out-of-school contexts can build the confidence students need when taking timed writing exams (Fisher, 2007). However, using socially and politically relevant issues allows students to access personal experiences and engage with multiple texts. And for Ms. Jane, this approach worked.

Pedagogical Portrait #2: "Who is your hero?" Cultural Relevance beneath the Surface

One February, Ellis had a mandatory Black History Month writing assignment for all students. The assignment, a citywide competition organized by a local organization, appeared on a flyer with vague instructions for students to write about a famous black American from their city who had a street named after her or him. There were no instructions about how to conduct the research on the streets' namesakes, nor was there a discussion about the writing process for such a project. Considering Ellis High School was more than 90 percent African American, the school's administration thought this Black History Month writing assignment would be well received. It was to be completed during Advisory; therefore, math, science, and social studies teachers, in addition to English teachers, were expected to assist students, whether or not these teachers were familiar with teaching writing. When the deadline came, more than half the student body showed up without an essay. Students who transferred to Ellis after leaving New Orleans in the wake of Hurricane Katrina resented the assignment that assumed their "heroes" were in their new city as opposed to the city they had to flee. Local students did not like the idea any better than their peers who transferred in from schools in New Orleans.

Mrs. Flowers, the ninth-grade literature teacher, joined the Ellis High School teaching staff after this failed attempt at assigning what the administration believed was a culturally relevant writing assignment. Moving beyond that attempt, Mrs. Flowers actively created a new project for the following year:

> For Black History Month, I wanted students to get away from Dr. King and Rosa Parks. No disrespect to them. I want[ed] them to understand that other African Americans have made contributions. I wanted them to dig deep into their families and into themselves and find someone who ignites their interests including musicians,

philosophers, etc. . . . [For this assignment], they got to interview their family members, teachers, or whomever they chose. They designed their own interview questions based on their interests. Final projects included Power Point presentations about The Negro League, Dorothy Dandridge—people who we know but who they were hearing about for the first time. Many of these interests came out of their interviews with family members.

When students interviewed family members and elders in their communities, they were introduced to some important figures in black history—through the memories and stories of people close to them. While Mrs. Flowers did foresee that students might have an opportunity to learn more about well-known black figures from their elders as they completed the assignment, she was pleased that it was the stories of their families that became the most compelling component of this assignment. Her "Who is your hero?" project, unlike the Black History Month essay assignment from the previous year, was received favorably by Mrs. Flowers's ninth-grade students. Students worked on preparing interview questions independently and eventually in small groups; all interview questions were posted on the class Blackboard so everyone in the class could share. Students had an opportunity to practice their interview techniques with each other before interviewing family and community members. Some of the questions students generated included "How was life different when you were growing up compared to now? What kind of music did you listen to? Who were your heroes?" These questions provided an opportunity for a cross-generational conversation where students had an opportunity to exchange information with interviewees.

When Mrs. Flowers joined Ellis, she was in her seventh year of teaching but new to the school district. After earning a BA in English, she completed a credential and master's degree program. Like Ms. Jane, Mrs. Flowers wanted to be at a school that had more of a "family environment" and believed SLCs had a better chance of achieving that than a large comprehensive high school would. Mrs. Flowers's beliefs about culturally relevant pedagogy in the writing classroom began in her teaching programs but became more pronounced during her pedagogical practice when she began to work at predominantly African American schools:

Culturally relevant teaching is asking the students for their expertise. The older I get the more I realize how out of touch I am with their music and television shows . . . I try to get them to see the writing process as something tangible for them and give them a plethora of writing assignments from persuasive essays to free verse poetry. Different students are stronger in different things. Like when [I] asked, "Who is your hero?" we explored this question while reading The Odyssey. Their hero could be their mom or someone at the corner store.

Mrs. Flowers and Ms. Jane shared the same philosophy about culturally relevant teaching. According to Mrs. Flowers, "The writing is about self-empowerment. They are at the age where they need to start to understand that they do have a choice about their futures. The decisions they make today have a direct impact on their future." Additionally, both teachers sought to use writers, topics, themes, and activities that helped their students become more confident readers, writers, and speakers. "Starting with culturally relevant topics," asserts Mrs. Flowers, served as a bridge to "more universal topics."

Pedagogical Portrait #3: "I just want to ignite them": Building Cultural Bridges through Writing

We recall an interesting conversation we had with another English teacher at Ellis after its first year as an SLC. The teacher commented that she wished she could introduce Latino heritage and culture to the students, including social studies and historical influences. Looking at each other incredulously, we asked in unison, "Why don't you? What's stopping you?" This teacher, a white American who had a great interest in Mexican, Central American, and Latin American history and cultures, responded, "Well, all the students are black so I guess. . . ." Her voice trailed off with concern her comments might be offensive, and perhaps counter to many people's perceptions of culturally relevant teaching: i.e., that culturally relevant teaching means inspiring students by centering the pedagogy on people who look like them and concerns that are readily connected to their experiences.

We understand how teachers sometimes arrive at this conclusion, and its counterpart: that because students are of a certain ethnic background, they will enjoy almost any piece of literature written by someone of that ethnicity. Maisha made this mistake early in her teaching career by assuming her tenth-grade literature classes—primarily African American students—would enjoy reading Richard Wright's *Black Boy*. As she created writing assignments and felt proud of herself for exposing students to Wright's work, an African American girl spoke up in class: "Why are we reading this? It's depressing! Can we read something positive about black people?" Our colleague, Bob Fecho, experienced a similar confrontation in his English class in a Philadelphia high school serving African American students. When Fecho read Nikki Giovanni's poem "Beautiful Black Men" with his students, he noticed a "terseness" in their responses. Finally, one student spoke up and declared Giovanni's poem was "making fun of the way Black people talk," forcing Fecho to realize that everything educators may deem relevant may not initially inspire students (2004, p. 13).

We have learned that students do not always like to read certain literature solely because the author shares the same ethnicity, religion, or gender—although at times that approach is valuable. We have also learned not all students want to write raps in English class just because they listen to hip-hop music in out-of-school settings. Part of culturally relevant pedagogy in writing instruction means we, as teachers and teacher educators, have to do more than introduce students to literature, social issues, and ways of writing that reflect students' own cultures. We also have a responsibility to expose students to worlds that initially look very different from their own through poetry, prose, film, and new words. By drawing upon themes that cross race, ethnicity, gender, and class and seeking other ways of demonstrating relevance, we can help students learn to care about topics and issues that arise in the lives of people who may not look like them or live where they live but with whom they share a global village. The challenge for teachers, then, is to find ways to create those cultural bridges.

Our work with preservice teachers pushed us to put these principles into practice. During the fall semester, Maisha asks the students in her Curriculum and Instruction in English course for the Masters in Arts in Teaching (MAT) program to create a curricular unit for Sandra Cisneros's *The House on Mango Street*. (This is a class in which we work together with preservice teachers, as Latrise is a teaching assistant who also supervises student teachers in their placements.) Cisneros's book of vignettes offers a good place for newer teachers to begin creating reading, writing, and speaking opportunities for middle and secondary students. In a study of a classroom teacher in a Chicago public high school who learned from his students, Michie (1999), for example, used *The House on Mango Street* to inspire some of his reluctant and struggling readers. A cadre of students in Michie's class even began to refer to themselves as the "Mango Girls" as they delighted in reading something that related to their lived experiences. Two student teachers, now classroom practitioners, who worked with Maisha and Latrise further developed ways to engage youth in writing through this vibrant book when they were student teaching at Ellis. However, both had very different experiences when they first introduced *The House on Mango Street*, experiences that pushed our thinking about culturally relevant pedagogy in the literacy classroom.

Ms. Luz was ecstatic about introducing ninth graders at Ellis to *The House on Mango Street*. When Ms. Luz joined the team, Ellis was in its third year and seeing more Mexican American students join its student body, even though it remained more than 90 percent African American. Prepared with a well-organized curricular unit featuring *The House on Mango Street* as the anchoring text, Ms. Luz began introducing the book's protagonist, Esperanza, to students. Mrs. Flowers, who was her cooperating teacher, did her best to let Ms. Luz develop a rapport with student without getting in her way. After hearing a few moans and groans, one of

Ms. Luz's students inquired why they had to read a book about a Mexican family. Ms. Luz, who was of Cuban descent, took great offense to the students' rejection of exploring any aspect of Latino cultures and came to us for support, advice, and just to vent:

> It just so happened that I was scheduled to begin my unit on *The House on Mango Street* at the end of February. I had big plans for the novel seeing as though I could relate to it and I had become very passionate about the vignettes. The very first day I introduced the novel I hit a figurative brick wall. I was prepared with my PowerPoint as well as supplemental materials and got as far as "We're about to start a novel called *The House on Mango Street* by a Mexican American woman named—" I was cut off by a question from a young lady—"Why are we learning about Mexicans when we're in Black History Month? It's NOT Cinco de Mayo!"

Because too many students had become so accustomed to only reading authors, literature, and work that mirrored their own lives, they were in many ways ambivalent about thinking about other cultures. Many of their teachers had embraced the term *culturally relevant* in a fairly limited way—e.g., giving students models of characters they will be familiar with—and the students picked up on this way of thinking. However, we believe this strategy of familiar models alone is not enough. Ms. Luz's experience shows that students can too easily be entrenched in what one scholar has called Multiculturalism 101: Heroes and Holidays (Banks, 2007). "Cultural logos" can be limiting when used as a sole lens to view particular groups (McHenry & Heath, 1994). When students believe that certain people can only be "read" or "studied" on certain days, then they have already missed the point in culturally relevant teaching.

One way to reach the students, perhaps, is to find links between their cultures and the cultures of others. Maisha and Ms. Luz sat down to do some planning and map ways to demonstrate links between African and Latino cultures. One of the things they shared was travel experience in Spanish-speaking countries where there is an African influence in the language, culture, music, and food. Together, Maisha and Ms. Luz created a curricular unit examining Afro-Latino music traditions. Students viewed the documentary *Under the Radar* (Branch, 2005) and participated in musical learning stations including the Afro-Peruvian singer Susan Baca (students sang Baca's songs for the rest of the day), Cuban hip-hop artists Buena Vista Social Club, and Orishas's "Music across the Seas." Students were also introduced to the photography of Antony Gleaton and specifically his series of portraits entitled "Tengo Casi 100 Anos," celebrating Africanism in Latin American countries. Ms. Luz also decided to ask students to compose "I am from" poems, adapting her lesson plan from Christensen's *Reading, Writing, and Rising Up*. Students created lists for categories such as "Things found in your home/yard," "Sayings/proverbs used by family members," "Names of relatives who link you to your past," "Foods that remind you of home," and a "Create your own category." All of these categories were individually represented on large poster paper throughout the classroom, and students were invited to post their responses on brightly colored sticky notes they added to the posters. From there students had the option to create an "I am from" poem using "I am" or "I am from" to begin each line. Students who found this scaffold too confining had the option of arranging the piece the way they saw fit. The "I am from" poem was a turning point. Once students created these pieces, Ms. Luz was able to build bridges between where students were from and where the character Esperanza was from and, in so doing, build bridges between different cultures and ethnicities.

Like Ms. Luz, Ms. Iman was a student teacher at Ellis. Ms. Iman attended undergraduate college in the area and wanted to teach in urban schools. Her desire to introduce her students to Esperanza in Cisneros's book was based in her firm belief in the power of exposure. Ellis students, according to Ms. Iman, may have lived in a cosmopolitan city but they spent most of their time in their segregated neighborhoods:

> These students were as culturally isolated as students in a rural Appalachia area . . . which means I had to be the representative, if you will, of the culture I was introducing through the literature. So with [*The House on Mango Street*], I studied Mexican American culture including art, music, history because I knew students had a superficial understanding. . . . [T]hey did not know what "Latino" meant or [how to] differentiate between the many groups.

Pushing her students to "differentiate" between the many Latino groups in the United States was timely. There were some miscommunications in the school between Mexican and African American students, miscommunications that were based on ignorance and lack of dialogue. Media coverage of Mexican immigrants only hindered the potential for communication and understanding. Aware of "the danger of a single story" (Adichie, 2009), Ms. Iman carried the potential for using *The House on Mango Street* to encourage students' multiple stories when she later moved out of state to claim her first full-time teaching job in the northeast. Ms. Iman's ninth graders at a diverse high school serving African, African American, Latino, and Asian students wrote vignettes on the following themes emerging from the text: first love; teenage memories you won't forget; me/who I am; and experiences with poverty or injustice. Ms. Iman's ninth graders produced a culminating project, *A Story All Our Own: An Anthology*, which included a collection of vignettes addressing these issues:

> You give the students an opportunity to express what it is they have to say. . . . [I]n sort of more traditional strategies when it is narrow and it does not include multiple

culture[s] and perspectives . . . students try to cajole their voices to match the standard so if you eliminate a standard to write about, you take a road block out of the way. Your voice, who you are is relevant and let me help you express it instead of, "No, you can't talk about this. This is not valid." You are saying, "You have a perspective. You are a writer. Everything you have is inside of you. . . ."

Using Cisneros's vignettes as a starting point, the students in Ms. Iman's class brainstormed and wrote their own vignettes. One student, Lucy, focused on using figurative language to show as opposed to tell her "teenage memory":

Student Writing Sample #1: A Teenager's Memory You Won't Forget (Lucy)
These thoughts are running through my mind, "We're going to lose. We can't win." I was scared. Taking baby steps we entered the gym. I could feel my temperature rising. There were so many faces I couldn't recognize all of them. I stepped into the court. The sweat falling down my yellowish-tan face. I grabbed the ball and I'm running as fast as I can, I get to my side and I take a shot. . . . I missed.

Another student, Azul, chose to write about her Quinceañera experiences:

Student Writing Sample #2: "Quinceanera" (Azul)
March 29, 2008, was the perfect day . . . the sun was looking at me with its big round glow. Tulips blooming on a spring morning. Birds singing and a little girl overwhelmed to become a young woman. It was my day. . . .

Ms. Iman also gave students prompts they could respond to including "experiences with poverty" or "being [enter ethnicity] in America." These prompts resonated with some students more than others, so Ms. Iman made sure she had many options.

Student Writing Sample #3: "Experience with Poverty" (Leona)
I can't. I can't think. All I do is stare. Stare into my life which is like on-going pain. Watching people's feet pound on [the city's] hard pavement. I can still hear the slaps of my father's hands against my mother's cheek. . . . As I stare in my future I realize that I don't have one.

Every student received a copy of the class anthology. By creating this anthology, students not only felt an immense sense of pride in their work but also in the work of their peers. Students learned about their classmates through the writing process in new ways that may not have happened and, again, learned to see across the personal to the more global.

What Do These Pedagogical Portraits Tell Us?

Narratives from classrooms and teachers are at once personal to those teachers and classrooms and purposeful in how they help others of us come to new and fuller understandings. These particular stories of four exceptional practitioners teach us a

lot about the role culturally relevant teaching played in their lives and the connections they were able to make between culturally relevant teaching and the teaching of writing, lessons that can help us think more fully about our own work with
students. Among the many lessons we learned from them are the following:

1. *Culturally relevant pedagogy in the English language arts classroom
includes socially and politically relevant issues in the lives of urban youth.* Students in Ms. Jane's class had an opportunity to research police brutality
cases nationally after students expressed concern about police brutality
in their communities. A series of activities designed to study this relevant
issue helped the students become stronger readers and writers: discussing issues out loud in class, using writing to hold virtual discussions on
Blackboard, conducting research under the guidance of teachers, reading
newspaper articles, following current events, learning new vocabulary
words, writing essays, and making connections beyond the classroom
(such as inviting a musician to class and reporting on the experience
to the rest of the school). Many of these activities are regular parts of
forward-looking writing classrooms; however, situating them in issues of
immediate concern to the students gave them new life.

2. *Dialogue, discussions, and orality in general are critical components
for writing and, indeed, are a part of the writing process and vital to culturally relevant teaching.* Discussion was essential in all classes, especially for
students who initially felt less comfortable as writers. Honoring students'
casual ways of talking in the language of conversation encouraged them
to think more deeply and more critically about important issues. This
increasing comfort with ideas and analysis then helped them realize they
had real ideas to offer that could make their way into writing. And when
teachers invited students to talk not only with their peers but with their
families and community elders, as Mrs. Flowers did in the Black History
Month project, students began to value the ideas and lessons that began
in their own communities. When teachers and schools value the ideas of
students' home communities and encourage students to bring those ideas
into the school setting, students can make greater connections across
their lives.

3. *Technology offers legitimate spaces for students to prewrite (e.g., Discussion Board on Blackboard, blogging, etc.):* While Ellis SLC has a technology focus, many schools are utilizing tools such as Blackboard and
blogging in their effort to meet the needs of students in the twenty-first
century who are experiencing technology in nuanced ways. The critical
part of using technology is that students have a legitimate place to begin
the writing process without having to focus on conventions at first. In
addition, the Internet has become an important source for disseminating
information when mainstream media may not cover particular stories.
For a culturally relevant classroom, this takes on great importance. Finding the stories that speak to students' concerns and finding outlets for

student voices to share with others what they've learned connects culturally relevant teaching to technology and writing. While research and
sharing of ideas certainly can be accomplished with pen and paper, using
technology in creative ways speaks to the worlds in which these students
live. A culturally relevant writing classroom, then, makes use of various
forms of media and various tools for writing and helps students become
familiar with these outlets.

4. *Culturally relevant writing assignments must be more than students
writing about shared ethnic and cultural backgrounds but also involve exposure
to new worlds, new people, and new ideas. The writing, then, becomes a bridge
between those worlds.* For example, Ms. Iman and Ms. Luz's classrooms
challenged their largely African American classes to consider the lived
experiences of Latino immigrants in the United States. Through reading,
music, art, and writing, Ellis students were exposed to different cultures
and thus learned to become open. In the process, many students saw
connections between their lives and the life of Esperanza in *The House
on Mango Street*. Later, Ms. Iman used the same text with white, Asian,
Black, and Latino students who used it as a blueprint to introduce and in
some capacity reintroduce themselves to their peers.

Culturally relevant instruction in the writing classroom is situated in—but
not limited to—the experiences of the students in the contexts in which we teach.
In the next chapter, we delve into this further as we offer ways to scaffold this kind
of pedagogy. We'll revisit these pedagogical portraits, pulling out specific strategies
these teachers used and situating those strategies within a discussion of instructional moves teachers can make to promote culturally relevant writing instruction.

Notes

1. All names are pseudonyms.
2. The author of the article, Paul Craig Roberts, worked with the Reagan administration and was a former *Wall Street Journal* editor.

Chapter Four

Let the Music Play: Culturally Relevant Writing Instruction

We have always loved writing. Latrise used to scribble in notebooks and journals when she was younger and still keeps a journal in her purse to jot down her musings. Maisha once carried a crate of personal journals to her tenth-grade English class, including the journal she had written when she was sixteen, chronicling the first time she visited New York City. When we taught high school, we enjoyed modeling writing for our students and finding ways to maintain cultural, political, and social relevance in our classrooms that kept up with the pace of our students' lives. Elsewhere, Maisha argues that English language arts teachers must be *practitioners of the craft*. In other words, English language arts teachers should be readers and writers; they should always be able to share something they are reading with students and colleagues, and they must be brave enough to share drafts of their writing the same way they ask students to share (Fisher, 2005a, 2005b, 2007, 2009). Engaging in these practices has given us great humility in our work with both youth and emerging teachers.

In Chapter 3, we concluded with a reflection on what we consider to be the most important qualities of a culturally relevant approach to teaching writing. In essence, we believe that culturally relevant writing pedagogy begins by helping students build bridges between their perspectives, ideas, and experiences even while we are teaching a very important skill. Many thoughtful teachers might argue that this is what they do already—and we would agree that much of what we would consider culturally relevant writing pedagogy is situated in what we know is good writing pedagogy in the first place. After all, many teachers—whether they consider themselves to practice culturally relevant pedagogy or not—have stories of trying to infuse students' perspectives, ideas, and experiences as they teach writing, in essence, to do whatever is necessary to appeal to their students' interests. Teaching writing well, some might say, is complex enough without adding another element.

However, we believe that culturally relevant writing pedagogy goes one step further: to help students learn to see how their own experiences, ideas, and perspectives can—in dialogue with others—give them a window into the social and political issues that impact their lives. This approach, we argue, can enhance the teaching and learning process for all teachers and students—whatever their race, gender, ethnicity, or social class. To exemplify what we mean and to offer some specifics about how to create a culturally relevant writing classroom in your own setting, we look, in this chapter, at the strategies the practitioners in the previous chapter employed as well as demonstrate some additional strategies we have used in our own classrooms, in our work with preservice teachers, and in workshops for experienced teachers in the teaching of writing.

In many ways, this chapter serves as a road map for teachers who want to implement these strategies in their writing instruction and teacher educators who aim to provide emerging writing teachers strategies for building and sustaining a culturally relevant curriculum. While we do not employ a traditional lesson plan format or a list of do's and don'ts for "what you should do to be more culturally relevant," we do offer ways to set the stage for learning, suggest "lead-in" strategies, and introduce inquiry-driven questions—that is, open-ended questions that invite students to consider multiple perspectives that inevitably lead to more writing opportunities. To begin this work, we revisit *NCTE Beliefs about the Teaching of Writing*, connecting that document to the work of culturally relevant writing pedagogy. Next, we provide an overview of some steps we have created for teaching writing in a culturally relevant way—using a music metaphor that reflects our interest in culturally relevant teaching and learning: "creating a playlist, managing content, syncing, and sharing." We then expand upon these steps in the context of Ms. Jane's, Mrs. Flowers's, Ms. Luz's, Ms. Iman's, and our own classroom communities. Here we seek to illuminate the work of Ms. Jane and her persuasive writing curriculum using the topic of police brutality, Mrs. Flowers's "Who is your hero?" project, and the work of Ms. Luz and Ms. Iman with *The House on Mango Street*. As you'll see, we contend that culturally relevant pedagogy in the writing classroom must include social and political relevance as well as what we consider best practices in the teaching of writing.

Teaching Writing in a Culturally Relevant Classroom

Like learning to write, learning to teach writing is a process. And though it is our belief that students benefit merely from having the opportunity to write, we know that good instruction matters. According to *NCTE Beliefs about the Teaching of Writing*:

> Whenever possible, teachers should attend to the process that students might follow to produce texts—and not only specify criteria for evaluating finished products, in form or content. Students should become comfortable with prewriting techniques, multiple strategies for developing and organizing a message, a variety of strategies for revising and editing, and strategies for preparing products for public audiences and for deadlines. In explaining assignments, teachers should provide guidance and options for ways of going about it. Sometimes, evaluating the processes students follow—the decisions they make, the attempts along the way—can be as important as evaluating the final product. At least some of the time, the teacher should guide the students through the process, assisting them as they go. Writing instruction must provide opportunities for students to identify the processes that work best for themselves as they move from one writing situation to another.
>
> Writing instruction must also take into account that a good deal of workplace writing and other writing takes place in collaborative situations. Writers must learn to work effectively with one another.

In other words, the process of teaching writing should include teachers identifying specific goals for students, yet at the same time providing both flexibility and opportunities for students to collaborate, share, and exchange. Good writing instruction also considers both process and product, helping students not only experiment with ways of writing but also commit to products that are audience ready. Teachers should create writing instruction that fosters the skills of developing writers as well as provides opportunities for their voices, perspectives, and experiences to become text. Also, teachers must make students aware that good writing comes out of multiple purposes and thus may require that students work collaboratively with others to identify and fulfill those purposes.

Though teachers may have multiple strategies for teaching writing that honor these beliefs, here we attempt to devise steps that allow for the process of teaching writing in ways that are culturally relevant and responsive. As we mentioned above, we use the language of music to map this journey. Music is our metaphor because, like our professions, music accommodates multiple genres and ways of creating, interpreting, and performing these genres. We honor the multiple teacher and classroom pedagogical portraits and provide strategies for how teachers can do this in their own classrooms. Our hope is that every teacher, teacher educator, and instructional leader reading this work will hear his or her own music and also be willing to create new music as well.

Steps for Teaching Writing in a Culturally Relevant Manner

1. *Create a playlist.* The first step in the process of teaching writing is to consider subject matter, curriculum, and genre. Teachers should connect writing activities to what students are expected to know (i.e., state, national, and local standards and individual teacher expectations) as well as students' own experiences. For example, Ms. Jane, in Chapter 3, used what students were expected to know—how to write persuasively—in tandem with students' experiences, reading, and concern about police brutality. Teachers should consider making a playlist that names both content to be taught and genres that students are expected to master that have the potential to connect to and even impact students' lives. Usually, specific state curriculum standards outline subject matter, curriculum, and genres that students are expected to experience in certain courses. However, when teaching writing, teachers should survey other related resources in order to make culturally relevant connections, as well as pose the kinds of questions that prompt intellectual thought and dialogue that later manifest into student writing. How teachers can actually begin to do this is outlined later in this chapter.

2. *Manage content.* Next, teachers should provide students with literature, media, and examples that can inform their writing. Ideas can be generated and inspired by reading articles and engaging in dialogue. Teachers are not limited to resources provided by schools. With the amount of technology available at our fingertips, teachers can explore the worlds of their students, find content that is culturally relevant, and create opportunities for students to be inspired to write by the world around them. Later, we explore how teachers can use several resources, including websites like ReadWriteThink. Ms. Jane, for example, used articles on police brutality as well as allowed the students to engage in dialogue via a classroom blog. Before they were expected to write, Ms. Jane provided an opportunity for students to *engage* content (reading) as well as *create* content (dialoguing) that informed their own ideas and infused their writing.

3. *Sync.* The third step is to sync your ideas with your students' ideas to fuel students' writing. While this includes providing feedback and making comments about students' writing, it is not limited to that. Syncing here means finding ways to introduce specific strategies for

writing instruction that meet students where they are—which is a cornerstone for culturally relevant writing instruction. In this step, teachers draw from students' funds of knowledge and build curriculum around student expertise. Examples of how teachers can make connections and provide feedback that go beyond written feedback are illustrated later in this chapter.

4. *Share your music.* Finally, teachers help students understand the public nature of writing by sharing a central part of the classroom. Teachers should begin this by writing alongside their students. When teachers model writing and experience the writing process with their students, they demonstrate how good writing is a process that takes time. Students also need to see that there are ways to become better writers. Providing examples of your own writing—that is, sharing drafts throughout the process, getting feedback, making revisions, etc. —is a wonderful means of taking the mystery out of producing writing. Likewise, students should be provided the opportunity to share their writing—especially in the kinds of nontraditional formats that will appeal to a wide variety of students. Performing writing, for example, creates community and instills ownership and pride in one's work. Students can compile anthologies, engage in public readings, publish work on the Internet, and write for school newspapers or class newsletters. Providing students with spaces to share their writing will give them a real audience and a sense of purpose.

The following sections provide examples of how classroom teachers can use culturally relevant pedagogy alongside writing instruction. While we draw from the pedagogical portraits of teachers in the previous chapter, we also expand from these examples in order to offer a robust view of writing in the culturally relevant classroom in real time. We illustrate how the teaching of writing and the writing process evolved in their classrooms using this musical metaphor. More specifically, we encourage teachers to create playlists, manage content, sync, and have students share their music. Later, we provide explicit guidance and resources for applying the process to create lessons related to particular curricula, genres, and texts.

Culturally Relevant Writing Instruction in Action

Example 1: Police Brutality in Ms. Jane's Class

Throughout the police brutality/persuasive writing unit, Ms. Jane's classroom was active and bustling. Cadres of students read and discussed articles while others used various media outlets to research news reports. One of our favorite days during this curricular unit was when Ms. Jane demonstrated to students how persuasive writing could take many forms, as she invited a local singer and songwriter, Anthony David, to class to perform his song "Krooked Kop." David's style, a mix of folk and R&B, was new for many of the students who, later in the unit, analyzed his lyrics

---

Questions to Ask Yourself in Creating Your Own Culturally Relevant Writing Classroom

Creating playlists:

- What are the content expectations (of my school, district, or state) for writing?
- What are my students' experiences with those expectations? Are some genres more familiar to them than others?
- What are my students' concerns, interests, and questions about their lives?
- How can I connect all these things?

Managing content:

- What kinds of resources can I find to help connect my students' interests to the curricular requirements?
- What strategies can I employ to keep students in dialogue with their reading? With each other? With bigger issues?

Syncing:

- What can I do to help students become successful writers?
- How can I provide useful feedback?

Sharing your music:

- How can I share my own writing with my students?
- How can I help students safely share their writing with their peers?
- How can I create conditions for students to share their writing more publicly?
- How can I introduce nontraditional genres for sharing while still meeting the curricular guidelines that I'm required to cover?

---

as a form of persuasive writing. Mr. David's relaxed style (he arrived to school on his bicycle because "it was a beautiful day so why not?") and his commitment to fighting for social justice inspired students. All of the carefully chosen teaching that occurred during the semester moved several students to create a newsletter for the rest of the Ellis student body sharing their experiences with Mr. David and the police brutality persuasive writing unit.

Elsewhere, Maisha writes about how high school English teachers use current events, and local events in particular, to inspire and motivate students to write (Fisher, 2005a, 2005b, 2007, 2009). Like Ms. Jane and Mrs. Flowers, teachers in schools throughout the country are looking for more authentic writing opportunities for their students. For example, classroom teacher and literacy coach Mama C, discussed in the previous chapter, used similar pedagogical practices as Ms. Jane and Mrs. Flowers. When Mama C's students in a high school writing circle learned about a young man in their peer group being shot and killed by a security guard on the rooftop of his apartment building when he was unarmed and only trying to leave his building to go next door, they were angry and frustrated (Fisher, 2009). Mama C wanted her students to transform their rage into poetry and prose that could be read at public forums and on community radio programs, mobilizing efforts to reevaluate security personnel procedures. Similarly, Ms. Jane invited her students to research and explore police brutality and the role it played in their lives as well as the lives of people throughout the United States. How did she make it happen?

Create Playlist

As we mentioned in Chapter 3, Ms. Jane began her class focus on police brutality with a local case brought to her attention by the concerns of her students, a case involving a young man known to students in the school. We strongly recommend beginning with local circumstances, as Ms. Jane did, such as an incident with which the students are familiar, and then moving to local newspapers and periodicals and finally extending the search to a national focus—moving from the local to the more global. As Ms. Jane moved the discussion outward—beyond the immediate circumstances to look at the bigger picture—she introduced the case of Oscar Grant in Oakland, California. She could have included readings on any number of cases, as there are, unfortunately, many similar incidents that students motivated by this topic can examine. Perhaps one of the more well-known police brutality cases that shocked our nation was the murder of Amadou Diallo. Diallo, a West African immigrant, was murdered in his doorway as he reached for his keys. The New York Police Department shot Diallo forty-one times, a case that ignited hip-hop artists and poets to write music, perform, and organize to bring awareness to police brutality. Writings surrounding this incident and many others would fit into this particular unit.

While this particular issue was of immediate significance to Ms. Jane's class, there will probably be other issues that matter greatly to others' students. And because persuasive writing is a consistent benchmark in secondary school writing curriculum, asking students to develop and refine an argument is a worthwhile skill that they will need in college. One way teachers can determine student interests—and thus a significant topic to pursue with them—is by engaging youth in participatory action research projects. For example, students can generate research questions on a topic they care about, collect data through qualitative interviews and field notes, and learn to analyze data and write up their findings. By drawing upon students' knowledge and life experiences to determine the topic under study, teachers can create a richness in a classroom community, one that successfully connects required content expectations, students' understanding of those expectations, and students' own interests and concerns about the communities in which they live. More specifically, "critical youth engagement" invites youth to engage in research with adult allies seeking "collective action for social change" (Fox & Fine, forthcoming). When students raise questions that address their lived experiences, then a more natural writing process grows out of inquiry and agency because writing leads to action.

While these approaches specifically reference the kind of social and political undercurrents that are common to a culturally relevant writing pedagogy, other less pointed approaches can be equally culturally relevant. One important approach for teachers to determine student interests is through developing what Nancie Atwell (1998) refers to as "writing territories." Writing territories give students a chance to identify topics and genres that they would like to write about and therefore can help young people understand that writing can be used for a variety of purposes, thus presenting writing as a lifelong journey as opposed to a classroom assignment. We also believe that asking students to develop reading territories and thinking territories is equally important. Generating reading territories helps students consider the pieces and genres of literature they would like to engage and helps them diversify their reading portfolios. Thinking territories are just that; students should have a space to brainstorm questions they have throughout the semester or academic year and topics they would like to focus on in the future.

One way to determine a topic for study—a topic that fits in with both curricular expectations and student interest—is to provide ways into discussion. An important question we always begin with is, "What is happening in your lives that you want to discuss/interrogate that relates to larger school/community issues?" Schools tend to restrict such activities to Advisory classes or after school programming; however, content courses can serve as a forum for students to engage these issues as well. More time that is spent on building and nurturing relationships through the writing process with students in the beginning of the academic year is less time wasted with management challenges throughout the semester. For example, in their study of process, product, and playmaking, Fisher, Purcell, and May (2009) demonstrate how relationship-building activities in their playwriting and performance workshops with incarcerated girls are really prewriting activities.

Teachers put a lot of pressure on themselves to create their own playlists in isolation when their best resources can be their students and their students' families. González, Moll, and Amanti (2005) assert that students and their families possess "funds of knowledge" including linguistic diversity and work experience that can be integrated into the classroom community. The best way to access students' and their families' funds of knowledge is to simply ask parents and students what skills and gifts they can contribute to class knowledge. This requires teachers

to take the time to get to know parents and guardians and make it a point to invite
them to the classroom.

Manage Content

Many teachers who wish to expand their curriculum in more culturally relevant
ways are not quite sure where to turn to find strong resources for their students.
Ms. Jane found one answer in resources developed by Kadiatou Diallo, the mother
of Amadou Diallo. Her memoir, *My Heart Will Cross This Ocean: My Story, My Son,
Amadou* (2004) chronicles her journey from Guinea to the United States as she
followed the American dream that so many immigrants believe in and work hard
to acquire. In conjunction with that memoir, she created a foundation in her son's
name that has resources and links to other websites and related organizations. Ms.
Jane used these resources and websites as a starting place for her students' research.

As students pursue culturally relevant topics and controversies, they need
their teachers to help them access articles selected from a variety of news sources,
including alternative media sources (local newspapers and listener-sponsored radio
programs). Inquiry-driven essential questions can support the kinds of reading
students are doing for this unit, immediately immersing students in writing as they
try to answer these questions:

- What is police brutality?
- Are law enforcement officers "above the law?" Why? Why not?
- What limits, if any, should law enforcement officers have when policing com-
  munities and neighborhoods?

Guiding students on this journey to find resources that will encourage thoughtful
analysis and discussion is an important role for teachers committed to this kind
of work. Students need to move beyond the emotional responses that can easily
dominate a discussion of issues so controversial and so close to their hearts. When
teachers like Ms. Jane help manage the content, ensuring students read from a
variety of perspectives, and provide them with guiding questions, students can then
develop a more critical stance toward the topic.

Sync

Finding ways to connect students' passions to the work of the class and use that
passion to fuel successful writing can sometimes be a challenge. However, using
the kinds of guiding questions that Ms. Jane created can help. Teachers can have a
dedicated space in the classroom for these guiding questions or they can be posted
on Blackboard and class websites for more technology-driven schools. Blackboard
websites, like the one Ms. Jane used in her class, offer a "discussion board" where

new "threads" can be introduced. Students can respond to each other as well as teachers. However, teachers can achieve this in their classrooms by posting the question on a bulletin board and supplying sticky notes for students. Another method is hanging butcher paper on the wall and inviting students to "tag" or respond to the questions that will also be posted publicly. These tags or postings should be left up for the duration of the curricular unit so that students and teachers can revisit them throughout the semester. Ms. Jane found that students were inspired to keep writing in this forum, trying to articulate their own ideas to their peers in response to the readings. This kind of writing served as a way to put their thoughts on paper, but also as a first step toward formulating the kinds of argument that would be key for their persuasive papers.

Another way Ms. Jane synced writing instruction to the study of police brutality was linking it to vocabulary study. As her students used writing to discuss articles and topics, they were at the same time developing a vocabulary for discussion. Recall, for example, that Ms. Jane's students studied the word "disenfranchised" prior to, during, and after their study on police brutality, using words from the unit for the Word of the Day. We encourage teachers to try this kind of approach or to require students to keep a journal in which they "catch" or "collect" words (Fisher, 2007), noting the definition, context, and their plans to use the words in their own writing. For example, in Poppa Joe's Power Writing seminar, students collected words in their journals from his original poetry (in which he strategically planted new words), during field trips (especially to museums and gardens), and from each other. This is teaching living, breathing vocabulary in context.

Share Your Music

Identifying final products at the beginning of this writing journey is essential. A portfolio is one idea for culturally relevant writing in classrooms—especially if the portfolios include multiple genres, some of which might reflect genres that are of particular interest to students. Portfolios can include:

- Persuasive essays written from different perspectives;
- Letters to editors of local, national, and global newspapers and periodicals with a focus on knowing one's audience; and
- At least one creative piece such as a play or spoken word piece. Playwriting introduces young writers to the art of dialogue, relationships, and problem solving (Winn, 2011). Spoken word pieces—or a strategic deviation from prose—can also provide students with the freedom to manipulate words, sounds, and literary devices that emulate their feelings about particular topics. *June Jordan's Poetry for the People: A Revolutionary Blueprint* (Jordan & Muller, 1995) has one of the clearest set of guidelines for a poem or spoken word piece, and *Brave New Voices: The Youth Speaks Guide to Teaching Spoken*

Word Poetry (Weiss & Herndon, 2001) offers exercises that build up to composing poetry and performances.

Ms. Jane asked her students to "share their music" by designing and writing a newsletter educating their peers about police brutality and sharing some of the learning experiences they had in her class. Her vision was that her tenth graders would disseminate the newsletter among the ninth graders to get them excited about the next school year.

When there is a potential to link between student writing and activism, we advocate multiple forums for interrogating topics. For example, Green's (2010) study of a youth radio community demonstrated the power of "air-shifting"—that is, "learning how to question, critique, and engage in social, political, and cultural discourse through radio programming." This is a great example of young people using writing for a variety of purposes and expanding to a genre that might appeal to particular students. In the context of this youth radio program, students research topics, write scripts, and prepare for interviews. Planning a radio program can be a final product (with or without an actual studio). We recommend that teachers who ask their students to create final products that move into unusual genres create specific questions for assessment, such as:

- What new ideas does this program generate about the topic?
- How does the program synthesize ideas presented in class discussions, readings, and independent research?

Perhaps an even more natural direction for introducing socially and politically relevant topics would be requiring students to prepare for a debate. Debate leagues teach critical writing skills through a process that involves collecting data (sometimes referred to as "buckets," referring to the physical containers holding all of the evidence one needs to support his or her point), analyzing and synthesizing data, and, of course, forming an argument and preparing talking points for a debate.

Example 2: Creating Relevance—Who Is Your Hero?

During the "Who/what is a hero?" project, students could be found designing interview protocols, struggling to work through interview transcripts and notes, and practicing interviewing techniques with fellow students. There was a real sense of agency in Mrs. Flowers's classroom throughout the tenure of this curricular unit; students worked independently as well as in small groups using their own judgment. Again, Mrs. Flowers wanted to steer clear of a coerced or obligatory Black History Month essay competition that asked students to research and write about given topics that often yielded half-hearted work. Mrs. Flowers's unit was more focused on the "living Black history" (Marable, 2006) that existed in students' neighborhoods, communities, families, and in some cases within the school walls, and on using this project as an impetus for ongoing writing.

Create Playlist

Mrs. Flowers set the stage for her "Who/what is a hero" project with an interactive bulletin that included students' "I am from poems," introduced by Ms. Luz. These poems included details of student lives: from words of wisdom espoused by family members and loved ones, to types of food that were reminiscent of family gatherings, to names of parents, grandparents, and other members of the family whom these young people adored. In sum, these poems demonstrated the cultural and linguistic diversity of students, a surprise to many in the class who thought they knew all there was to know about their peers. One of the next steps for students included generating a list of well-known people of African descent—including West Indians and Africans from the continent—they were interested in knowing more about. Students also identified individuals they could interview who might know more about these well-known people because they either grew up knowing their politics, listened to their music, or were influenced by them in some way. Some examples included a student interviewing her grandmother to learn what she remembered about Dorothy Dandridge and another student interviewing members of his family about their knowledge of the Negro Baseball League. For some students this was the extent of their project; they tried to get to know their subjects more intimately through the journey of someone closer in age or who lived during a particular era. However, other students became keenly interested in their interviewee, who in some cases was someone in the school or in their family.

Prior to Black History Month, Mrs. Flowers's students had recently finished *The Odyssey* and throughout this reading journey they raised many questions about who is considered a hero or heroine (as well as a discussion of the feminization of the word "heroine"). Students also raised questions about why particular pieces of literature were required at the high school level and who made such decisions. Mrs. Flowers used all of these seemingly tangential discussions as points of entry for creating the "Who/what is a hero?" project, modeling what culturally relevant pedagogy looks like in the writing classroom; student talk is woven into the fabric of the classroom and used to spur the creation of written texts. Initially, Mrs. Flowers did not see a connection between *The Odyssey* and honoring African American history during the month of February; however, listening to her students invited a new line of inquiry in her classroom. Students wanted to honor their own heroes as opposed to having heroes handed down to them; this yearning from students was the backdrop for this unit. Mrs. Flowers underscored that students were responsible for creating history; they were challenged with the task of identifying heroes who lived outside the so-called canon and learning as much as they could about these people so they could learn and share their stories.

Students were encouraged to conduct interviews and oral histories and, therefore, needed to create questions that were relevant and compelling. Before this exercise, many students did not realize how much research they had to do to prepare for an interview. Students also had to practice listening, knowing when and where to enter the interview and how to take notes simultaneously. Perhaps most challenging was mining these notes to construct a piece of prose they felt represented their subject. This project invited writing for a variety of purposes and introduced students to a toolbox they could use throughout their high school curriculum and beyond.

Manage Content

To begin this unit, students could explore "universal" heroes such as Mahatma Gandhi, Dr. Martin Luther King Jr., and Mother Teresa. How have they become heroes? What makes them heroes? Are heroes allowed to be flawed? Why or why not? We raise these questions because, much like the literary canon, there is also a canon of heroes or men and women who are generally celebrated without question. When Mrs. Flowers's students challenged her choice to include *The Odyssey* in her curriculum, she accepted the challenge by turning the questions around and asking students to not only question, critique, and challenge but also to be prepared to write new histories.

To help students think about what it means to document and write about an "everyday hero," resources such as documentaries, autobiographies, memoirs, and biographies about men and women—both famous and not so famous—should be available in the classroom library. Once students study this genre of writing, teachers can introduce alternative stories using resources like the Point of View (POV) series and series such as African American Lives and Black in Latin America that trace the genealogy of people both known and not so known. (While the Black in Latin America series was not produced when Ms. Luz student-taught in Mrs. Flowers's class, it would have been an excellent resource to use with *The House on Mango Street* as well, to show connections between people of African descent and people of Latin American descent.) Another important resource for writing up the stories of everyday people is the *New York Times'* "One in 8 million" article series; each article profiles a New York City resident and tells his or her story in ways that capture elements of surprise and delight. Such stories, the series makes clear, would otherwise go largely unnoticed.

We also like the idea of having students confront contemporary tensions in thinking about heroes. For example, students can brainstorm the ways in which famous people—especially musicians, actors, and athletes—are viewed as heroes or role models even if they do not position themselves as such. Retired NBA basketball player Charles Barkley presented an interesting idea about this very topic in the height of his career when he announced that he was not and should not be considered a role model. Many public figures disagreed with Barkley because they believed young people admired him merely because he was a popular basketball player, making him a role model whether he wanted to be or not. We would take this question to our students and invite them to grapple over it. Are heroes simply so because of their talent or are there other criteria? Why or why not? Is being a hero a choice? Why or why not? These kinds of questions can also bridge generational and social gaps between teachers and students who sometimes live in very different worlds.

Sync

Syncing and sharing complement each other in this curricular experience. Bringing local heroes to class or to the school during town hall meetings is one culminating event that strategically taps into students' funds of knowledge. Conducting oral histories as a classroom or schoolwide initiative will not only provide students with a meaningful and real world learning experience but can also be a community building activity that fosters nurturing relationships between students and their peers and students and teachers. Student Press Initiative (SPI), for example, has guides such as *Project Notes: Conducting Oral History in the Secondary Classroom* (McKibbin, 2005) and anthologies such as the Speaking Worlds series, which are oral histories that secondary students collected in various contexts. Throughout this unit, students are writing: writing questions prior to their interviews, writing notes during the interviews, and—of course—writing up their findings.

Share Your Music

Writing for this curricular unit can focus on many genres including memoir, biography, and journalism inspired pieces. Interviews can be published as a class set with commentary, reflections, or essays exploring the common themes in the interviews. While Mrs. Flowers used "Who is your hero?" as an extension of her unit on *The Odyssey*—which was required reading for ninth graders at Ellis—these activities still stand on their own. Here, culturally relevant teaching strategies provided a scaffold to a text that was part of the state's curriculum. We want to underscore the fact that building this scaffold does not undermine the work that precedes reading

The Odyssey. Educational research sometimes presents culturally relevant pedagogy as a bridge to learning canonical texts or making these texts more meaningful to students. We believe these student-generated texts can be used independently or be used in partnership with required reading for schools. At the end of this learning experience, students should be given an opportunity to extract information from interviews to focus on particular skills such as writing biography, integrating quotes in text, using signal phrase verbs, and crafting transitional sentences.

Example 3: Bridging Relevance—Esperanza and Cisneros

Ms. Luz and Ms. Iman were dynamic emerging teachers. Student talk was encouraged and expected in their classrooms. One might hear music spilling out of their classrooms and both new teachers were fearless when it came to utilizing multiple forms of media. They were the first to attempt to teach Sandra Cisneros's *The House on Mango Street* at Ellis and even though there were some bumps (and we believe bumps can be good!), these two teachers were able to expose students to a character who, they learned, they had more in common with than they initially thought. The character of Esperanza, a girl who yearns for a home she can be proud of, a home that will not invoke responses like, "You live *there*?" took literature classes throughout the United States by storm. Through a series of vignettes, Cisneros *shows rather than tells* the stories of Esperanza, her family, friends, and neighbors—an immediate representation of a basic tenet of writing instruction. As a piece of literature, *The House on Mango Street* both demonstrates content that speaks to the experiences of many young people and transcends ethnicity (a dream for a culturally relevant classroom) and serves as a model for excellent writing instruction. Ms. Luz and Ms. Iman used this book to demonstrate both points to their students.

Create Playlist

Vignettes in Cisneros's book do not have to be read in order. Teachers we work with often begin with a vignette that supports or extends other ideas explored throughout the year. In the vignette "Those Who Don't," readers learn about the ways in which people who live outside Esperanza's neighborhood view her community and its residents; that is, "those who don't" live in Esperanza's neighborhood generalize, stereotype, and often fear the people she sees as dynamic and who have storied lives. An interesting way of understanding this vignette and connecting it to the larger world is to help students see how Cisneros captures the ways in which people's language is often raced, classed, and gendered. To complement this reading, teachers might require students to analyze newspapers and/or news reports and search for the ways in which words and phrases are similarly coded for race, class, and gender. Writing about their findings either in a persuasive voice or using analytical writing tools would work well. Students can begin this writing activity by responding to essential questions such as:

- What is urban? What is rural?
- How are urban inner city communities described in the media?
- What is the evolution of words like "ghetto" or "barrio?" How have these words been raced, classed, and gendered?

Manage Content

In early editions of *The House on Mango Street*, an endorsement from Pulitzer Prize–winning poet Gwendolyn Brooks sits right under the title. Brooks's endorsement, yet another indication of how important Cisneros's work has become, inspired these teachers to use Brooks's work side by side with *The House on Mango Street*. Brooks's acclaimed *A Street in Bronzeville* (1945), for one, captures life in Chicago's "Black belt," which was an entirely African American section located on the south side of the city, and beautifully complements *The House on Mango Street*. While many teachers use *The House on Mango Street* alone, we believe there are many wonderful opportunities to merge this text with books like Brooks's and others. Quilter, artist, and children's book author Faith Ringgold, for example, illustrated a richly colorful edition of *Bronzeville Boys and Girls* (Brooks & Ringgold, 1956/2007) featuring the poetry of Brooks against the backdrop of Ringgold's art. We like the idea of having students read this book and then creating their own "cityscapes" and historiographies of their cities and communities. In these "cityscapes," students can use poetry, prose, and/or historical writing to unearth the cultural gems they have at their fingertips. (See more on this below.) Historians have demonstrated why particular neighborhoods and their changes over time matter for the rest of the country. These urban histories provide different researching and writing opportunities for students. Other choices for linking with other texts might be Judith Cofer's *An Island Like You* or Nikki Grimes's *Bronx Masquerade*. Literary theorist Veve Clark called this approach "Marassa consciousness," promoting the "twinning" of texts to forge more in-depth relationships with the characters and themes.

Sync

The House on Mango Street offers numerous opportunities for teachers to introduce lessons that can help with student writing. The "I am from" poems featured in Linda Christensen's *Reading, Writing, and Rising Up: Teaching about Social Justice and the Power of the Written Word* (2000) can serve as either a prewriting activity or an assignment unto itself and have become very popular in urban schools. We have witnessed students who had never picked up a writing utensil in their classroom take great pride in creating an original "I am from" poem. Maisha, for example, used this activity with ninth graders who were reading the *Autobiography of Malcolm X* and saw an entire middle school accept the "I am from" challenge, igniting a schoolwide writing spark.

Teachers can push this assignment further by asking students to contribute a vignette about their communities and neighborhoods to a class anthology project, a project that is used widely in classes reading *The House on Mango Street*. Ms. Iman's class did a variation of this project by creating cityscapes. In a cityscape, students are asked to research the history of their neighborhoods, which can include popular street names, specific buildings, as well as the evolution of the neighborhood with respect to race and class. In Kinloch's *Harlem on Our Minds: Place, Race, and the Literacies of Urban Youth* (2010), youth read about the gentrification, or what they refer to as the "whiteification of the hood" in their Harlem neighborhoods, as text. Not only did students write about their lived experiences with gentrification, but they also attended neighborhood meetings and joined coalitions to help save their communities.

Share Your Music

Ms. Iman's class anthology was not only a culminating project to build community; it was an opportunity for student to revisit their writing, make revisions, and publish. This gave Ms. Iman an opportunity to assess how student writing improved over time. Teachers can also encourage this kind of writing to go public. A cityscapes project could have a dedicated space (preferably a hallway or interactive bulletin accessible to all students and teachers). A more technology-rich school environment can upload projects and create a website for the school. Oral histories, discussed in conjunction with Mrs. Flowers's work, can also be integrated into the cityscape projects. The interdisciplinary nature of an urban history of a city provides access to many skills including research, oral history, synthesizing materials, using citations in writing, and reviewing multiple sources.

For the next section, instead of providing you with another example of how a particular teacher has done it in his or her own classroom, we attempt to illustrate the process more explicitly and provide resources that can help teachers get started with considering writing instruction that is culturally relevant in their own classrooms.

Let Your Music Play: Creating a Culturally Relevant Writing Unit

For this illustration, we begin with mandated curriculum. Unlike Ms. Luz, who begins with specific questions that guide her curricular unit, Ms. Jane, who is prompted by student interest, or Ms. Luz and Ms. Iman, who begin with a specific text, we hope to further illustrate how these "beginnings" can be used alongside curriculum—even mandated curriculum—to create culturally relevant learning and writing opportunities for your students.

Create Playlist

Because we live and work in Georgia, we'll start there. We do this knowing that while your state's content standards may be different, we're betting there are a lot of similarities. The Georgia Department of Education website suggests that students in the ninth grade should produce "writing that establishes an appropriate organizational structure, sets a context and engages the reader, maintains a coherent focus throughout, and signals closure" (Georgia Department of Education, 2006). This standard invites students to engage several genres of writing related to a myriad of subject matter. Given that standard, we would consider three ways to generate a playlist: (1) draw upon student interests and lived experiences, (2) determine which genres we want students to read and write, and (3) establish essential questions.

Students' Interests and Lived Experiences

To make students' interests a part of the playlist, teachers can survey students. This can be done in several ways. Teachers can find out what students are interested in by giving them either an open-ended or closed written survey. Teachers should not only pose questions about subject matter or learning styles, but should invite students to share experiences, resources, and ideas that are related to their lives. These written surveys are valuable in the beginning of the semester but can be useful if given several times throughout the year. Many administrations allow for the development of the "writing and thinking territories" we refer to earlier in this chapter. In addition to more general surveys, teachers can also begin each unit of study with a specific set of questions designed to find out not only how culturally relevant connections can be made in a particular unit, but also what students may already know about a particular subject matter, concept, or skill. We provide an example of a general interest survey in Figure 4.1. Teachers can modify it to meet more specific needs.

Figure 4.1. One example of a general interest survey.

Interest Survey

Name _____   Date _____

1. What types of things do you like to read?

☐ Novels   ☐ Newspapers   ☐ Plays

☐ Short stories   ☐ Stuff on the Internet (blogs, websites, etc.)

☐ Other narratives   ☐ Poetry

☐ Magazines   ☐ Essays

2. What was the last thing you read that you really enjoyed? Why?

_____

_____

_____

_____

3. What types of things would you like to read about in class?

_____

_____

_____

_____

4. What types of activities do you do outside of school?

☐ Sports   ☐ Music   ☐ Hang out with friends

☐ Drama   ☐ Video Games   ☐ Dance

☐ Social Networks (e.g., Facebook)   ☐ Family   ☐ Band

☐ Hair/Nails   ☐ TV   ☐ Other _____

5. Rate the type of writing you would rather do, "1" being your favorite and "4" being your least favorite.

_____ Narrative (Storytelling)

_____ Essay

_____ Poetry

_____ Reports

6. If you had to provide a title for your life story, what would it be?

_____

Genres Students Should Encounter

The next consideration for creating a playlist is noting which genres we want students to encounter or, better yet, which genres are required by state or national standards. Reading is such an important aspect of writing because books, magazines, etc. provide examples of what and how we want our students to write. We should thus provide ample opportunities for students to engage with multiple varieties of texts. For example, after surveying students' interests, a teacher may decide to incorporate several genres related to a particular theme or idea. A teacher may deduce that many of the students could relate to the idea of *life as an arena*, a space of personal struggle and conflict. Some students may relate to it literally, in that they may play sports. Others may be able to connect with a more metaphorical example such as struggling to graduate. School or home may be the arena for some. Students may share a connection with historical arenas, like the Civil Rights Movement.

Finding a variety of texts related to a subject matter that can yield such diverse connections can be a daunting task. However, it helps to keep in mind which genres students should encounter and that each student does not have to read and/ or respond to everything you find. According to Georgia Performance Standards, ninth-grade students should read biographies, autobiographies, novels, memoirs, poetry, short stories, plays, and editorials. Teachers can begin their search for related texts on websites like ReadWriteThink.org in order to find sample lesson plans, articles, and other resources by typing in key words.

Also, the matrix in Table 4.1 shows how teachers can keep track of the many genres students are engaging throughout the year. Latrise has used this in her class to make sure that each student is reading (and writing) the required genres without having to make students read all the same things at the same times. In other words, this chart is used throughout the year to maintain a log of each genre students are encountering.

As we mentioned earlier in this chapter, to engage students in culturally relevant writing, we would also do well to offer them the opportunity to explore other genres that are expressive of the communities and cultures in which they live and in which they make change. Spoken word poetry, for example, can sit side-by-side with more traditional poetry study; persuasive writing can take many forms—from op-ed pieces to blog entries to public service announcements.

Essential Questions

Posing questions is an important part of any classroom. Using essential questions to frame a unit can ensure that what students are learning is culturally relevant.

Table 4.1. Genre Matrix (Reading)

Student Name	Biography		Autobiography			Novel		Memoir		Short story				Poetry						Play		Editorial	
Student A			✓			✓				✓	✓													
Student B	✓									✓	✓	✓												
Student C	✓									✓	✓													
Student D						✓				✓				✓									✓	

Essential questions are questions that frame a unit of study. They are questions to be contemplated before, during, and after a unit. Essential questions connect local ideas (those from text and from students' experiences and dialogue) to global ones (ideas that influence culture, politics, technology, entertainment, etc.). The following sample essential questions that could be posed during this unit on "Life as an Arena" could be adapted to any kind of unit.

Unit: Life as an Arena: Conflict and Personal Struggle

Essential Questions:

What is an arena?

How can an arena be like life?

What is needed in order to have conflict?

Does there have to be conflict in an arena?

Manage Content

Now that you have created a playlist by considering your students' interests and lived experiences, noting what genres they should encounter, and posing several essential questions, it is time to manage content: that is, decide on specific readings and lessons plans that will allow students to produce specific types of writing. In order to do this, teachers should (1) identify specific texts students will engage, (2) consider what types of writing students will produce, and (3) create writing lessons that will teach students how to produce the types of writing that meet national and state standards.

Specific Texts That Students Will Engage With

One of the worst mistakes teachers can make is depending solely on school-issued textbooks to dictate what students will read throughout the year. Although we believe textbooks are useful, it is important to take advantage of available technologies to invite other voices into the classroom. Most of the time marginalized, local, young, and culturally relevant voices are omitted from traditional textbooks. So once you gauge which genres students should be experiencing, the next step is to find specific works that are relevant to your students. Keeping with the theme noted in the previous section—"Life as an Arena: Conflict and Personal Struggle"—there are several texts which could be included in a unit like this, as seen in Table 4.2.

Table 4.2. Possible Texts for the "Life as an Arena" Unit

Title/Author/Year of Publication	Genre	Grade levels
"In the Arena," Theodore Roosevelt, 1910	Speech excerpt	6–12
Push, Sapphire, 1996	Novel	10–12
The House on Mango Street, Sandra Cisneros	Novel	6–12
A Step from Heaven, An Na, 2001	Novel	6–12
Crick Crack Monkey, Merle Hodge, 2000	Novel	8–12
"Paisley Park," Prince	Song	
"One in 8 Million" *New York Times* series	Images/Interviews	6–12
"All the world's a stage," William Shakespeare	Monologue	9–12
Bridge and Tunnel, Sarah Jones, 2006	Play	
The Bluest Eye, Toni Morrison, 2006	Novel	8–12
"Charge of the Light Brigade," Alfred, Lord Tennyson, 1870	Poem	9–12

Teachers should remember that it is not simply the texts or activities that make up culturally relevant pedagogy. The connections that students are invited to make through their dialogue and writing also make up culturally relevant pedagogy.

Writing That Students Will Produce

Mandated curriculum, essential questions, anticipated dialogue, and texts can help teachers decide what type of writing students will produce and for what purposes. Each text that students engage is space for inspiration and modeling. While the possibilities seem endless, teachers should narrow each unit to a couple of major writing assignments and a project assessment so that students have time to engage the writing process. In a successful unit, students will write all along the way—responding to discussion questions, blogging about their ideas (and ideals), reflecting in journals, etc., an approach that matches the Georgia Performance Standards, which expect ninth graders to practice all modes of writing. In addition to daily journal writing, blogging, and answering questions posed throughout the unit, students might also be asked to produce at least two or three polished writing assignments. For the sake of this particular unit, teachers could have students produce a descriptive essay that is an extended metaphor that addresses the question: What type of arena best describes your life? Or students could create and perform a monologue in which they take on the roles of several characters dealing with personal conflict.

How is a teacher to keep up with all the types of writing students are producing over the course of a semester? Like the reading matrix mentioned earlier, a writing matrix can help to create a context in which teachers allow students to choose the types of writings they produce, while ensuring that they become proficient in a variety of types (see Table 4.3).

Writing Lessons

Before deciding on particular lessons, teachers should first consider what students need to know: that is, what particular skills are needed to produce a particular piece of writing. For example, for the descriptive essay mentioned in the previous section—What type of arena best describes your life?—students will need to know what an extended metaphor is and how to develop sensory details to be able to describe their own arenas. Here is a perfect opportunity for teachers to reference the texts that students have engaged during the unit. For example, students could discuss the main characters from many of the texts from the unit and describe their "arenas." Pecola, the protagonist in Morrison's novel *The Bluest Eye*, has to deal

Table 4.3. Genre Matrix (Writing)

Student	Essays				Creative Writing			Nonfiction/Technical	
	Expository	Persuasive	Descriptive	Narrative	Monologue	Short story	Poetry	Article	Research Paper
Student A	✓	✓						✓	
Student B		✓	✓	✓					✓
Student C	✓					✓	✓		✓
Student D	✓				✓	✓		✓	

with several conflicts (with her mother and father, with herself, and with society). Students could discuss Pecola's life as an arena. That is, students first describe the physical and metaphorical spaces that allow for such conflict while noting how the players (other characters) are involved. Here, students should point out sensory details from the text and create a log they can refer to for their own writing.

When teaching writing, it is important not to take on too much at one time. While explaining in detail how a lesson should be conducted is beyond the scope of this book, it is especially important to note that teachers are most successful when they focus on a particular writing strategy at a time, much as Nancie Atwell describes in her approach to mini-lessons. If teachers are teaching sensory details, for example, then that should be the focus of the reading, writing, and assessment related to that particular lesson.

Sync

Syncing ideas and making connections are important in any classroom, but especially when teaching writing. During this step of the teaching writing process, students and teachers are sharing ideas that can fuel students' writing. Syncing should not merely involve teachers providing written feedback, but instead should be an opportunity for teachers and students to discuss, critique, and build upon each other's work. Ways to accomplish this are to (1) make use of graphic organizers, and (2) allow students to critique and respond to one another.

Graphic Organizers

Needless to say, graphic organizers are especially helpful when writing. Graphic organizers help writers jot down ideas in a way that allows them to begin to consider content and organization. Usually, graphic organizers are personal and are seldom shared. However, Maisha and Latrise have used class graphic organizers to get students to share ideas and comment (sometimes in writing) on others' ideas. A class graphic organizer is usually a giant version of an individual one and students use sticky pad paper to share ideas with the class. For example, to introduce the idea of life as an arena, a teacher can pose several questions for students to consider in writing. Students post their answers and are provided time to read and respond to what other students wrote. This can also be done as a class blog. The most important thing is that the organizer should be a living document that students and teachers are allowed to visit in order to raise points, spark ideas, and add to as the unit progresses and as they compose their own writing.

Students Critique and Respond

We cannot stress enough how important student dialogue is in the classroom. Teachers should provide daily opportunities for students to grapple with the ideas that result from reading and writing text. With the type of teaching and learning that have been described above, students will have a chance to engage in the activities that will help them become better writers. In Maisha's earlier work with youth poets and writers in the Bronx, she described in ethnographic detail the "read and feed" process in Joseph Ubiles's or Poppa Joe's classroom. One student poet, Pearl, shared her haiku poetry and inspired dialogue among her peers:

> **Joe:** Pearl actually has a symphony. In how many movements? In six movements?
>
> **Pearl:** Five. I don't have them typed.
>
> **Joe:** But you have a succession of haikus. At some level repeated haikus or extended haikus are called Tanka, Waka, or Renga.
>
> [Pearl recites her poem.]
>
> **Yari:** It's strong in the beginning but then the high just tears up my heart. I was waiting for more—a usually happy ending.
>
> **Joe:** Feed her, Rob. What did she make you feel?
>
> **Rob:** I don't know.
>
> **Joe:** What did you hear? What music did you hear when she was reading? Did you hear any?

Rob: What do you mean?

Joe: If she was reading, what music would you play behind her?

Rob: Oh. "All My Life."

Joe: Does anyone know that song?

Joel: K-Ci and Jo Jo?

Pearl (singing the words): *All my life, I prayed for someone like you…*

Joel: I used to like it but then it got played out.

Joe: But did that serve you? Would you play that song?

Pearl (smiling widely): Yes, I would.

Joe: Okay, all right. Then that's a match.

Yari: That's a beautiful match.

Joe: Danielle?

Danielle: It was good.

Joe: Okay.

Aleyva: It makes me feel what she's saying. A lot of feelings.

Yari: I feel that way sometimes.

Joe: What do you feel?

Yari: I feel that way sometimes.

Joe [addressing Pearl]: Okay. All right. Now that's interesting. You know. See how strong [it is]? You got somebody who visited self.

Joel: How could I put it? In every person I think there's sort of that love, love [inaudible] and I feel like you portrayed it really beautifully with your haikus. Most of the time haikus are meant to be something—it really is meant to be a one-hitter quitter. But these didn't quit you in one hit. It flowed well. Even though the form wasn't meant for that. That's what I felt like it really just carries you in. It carries you like a road with hills. That's what I felt like. There were some high parts and then it let's you down but not down in the sense that it gets boring but in the sense that the excitement goes down a little. Just pay attention to detail. I felt like it was very nice.

Pearl: Thank you.

Joe: I feel like I won because you resisted haiku for so long but today you very deliberately in a very public forum decided not only to read a very intimate thought but to use a form that you really weren't happy with in the beginning. And now I think you see the efficiency in the form. So my grievance was 'cherry lips' but 'juicy lips' works for me. [Laughter]

Yari: It gives it taste. (Fisher, 2007, pp. 24–25)

The read and feed process invites students to read their original work and learn how to give and receive critical and specific feedback. Teachers are a part of the read and feed process; they wait for students to "feed" each other first and then they offer a feed as well. Read and feed embodies the sync and share mechanisms of culturally relevant writing pedagogy.

Share Your Music

The final step to the teaching writing process invites students and teachers to share their writing—in traditional and nontraditional formats. Here, students and teachers experience the writing process. Students are provided ample opportunity to engage models of good writing, discuss the content and format of good writing, and create good writing. There are several ways in which students and teachers can share their writing. When planning to share "music," teachers should consider designating time during class for sharing and setting specific guidelines for sharing.

In the next chapter—which focuses on assessment—we suggest ways and spaces in which students and teachers can share their music. In addition, we discuss the ways teachers can assess the dynamic writing that emerges from culturally relevant pedagogy. One thing we see and have been guilty of in our own teaching is introducing creative and compelling assignments but relying on static measures for achievement. Chapter 5 attempts to offer new ways of thinking about assessment in the culturally relevant writing classroom.

Chapter Five

From Gold to Platinum: Assessing Student Writing

Assessing students' writing can be a difficult undertaking. Before we became strategic assessors, the ways we provided feedback and graded work could have been described as arbitrary and even haphazard. We corrected grammar mistakes and errors in usage and mechanics, and suggested "better" ways to word sentences. Students' papers were marked with red ink, a letter grade was assigned, and students were given feedback that allowed for some improvement. Many students simply took their papers and placed them in their notebooks, never to look at them again. Were they becoming better writers? Perhaps somewhat better, if only because they were writing a lot. However, we realized we were overlooking an opportunity to take students' writing from gold to platinum, a feat to be accomplished only by careful, consistent, and deliberate assessment.

Mastering a process for assessing writing takes commitment and planning. However, it is doable and necessary. We believe that in order to help all students become effective writers, there are certain practices that must be a part of our teaching and learning process. In Chapter 2, we defined culturally relevant pedagogy as humanizing, respectful, and considerate of the histories, perspectives, and experiences of students as an essential part of the subject matter, classroom practices, and content of educative practices and spaces. Culturally relevant pedagogy considers students' experiences as legitimate and official content of the classroom curriculum. In this chapter we show ways teachers can use thoughtful writing assessment as a way to continue the tenets of culturally relevant pedagogy—that is, to create meaningful learning opportunities for students while fostering academic success, inviting students' cultural competencies, and developing students' critical consciousness.

In the following sections, we discuss classroom practices that account for both culturally relevant pedagogy and effective writing instruction, provide examples of how assessment of such practices can be integrated alongside culturally relevant pedagogy, and suggest products that could result from such instruction. While we talk some about formal writing assessment, you'll notice that much of what we suggest falls into the category of informal or formative assessment. Informal writing assessment, we argue, is particularly important in a culturally relevant classroom because of its role in helping teachers identify student strengths and challenges along the way, thus giving teachers timely information that can help students continually improve.

We begin by looking at the connections between culturally relevant writing instruction and ways to effectively assess students' writing, pointing to some specific classroom practices and how teachers might assess students' learning in those situations. Then, we take on the informal assessment, assessment with a little *a*, which refers to the daily assessment done by teachers during writing instruction in order to evaluate what students can do and which areas require additional instruction and support. Next, we discuss more formal examples of Assessment, assessment with a big *A*, which summarizes ways teachers can assign grades and feedback using rubrics, projects, and formal writing tasks. Finally, we conclude with thoughts on how all of this plays out in a culturally relevant classroom.

Assessing Writing Instruction That Is Effective and Culturally Relevant

Teachers often assess students' writing according to a standard set of rules commonly associated with "Standard English." This approach is certainly useful in that teachers want to and should provide their students with the skills and language that will afford them certain opportunities and access to social, political, and economic institutions. Academic success is dependent on one's ability to master the literacies of school. However, culturally relevant pedagogy insists that one language is not upheld over another, that different languages simply serve different purposes, a stance promoted by many scholars and made practical in NCTE's well-known

Students' Right to Their Own Language (Conference on College Composition and Communication of NCTE, 1974). In an article revisiting that document, Kinloch (2005, p. 104) offers English language arts educators a new lens through which to view the scholar activism of Geneva Smitherman and June Jordan. In an effort to promote democratic engagement among students and honor linguistic diversity, Kinloch suggests a variety of activities to help preservice teachers understand the implications of that work, activities that can also be used in culturally relevant writing classrooms:

- Students can be involved in participatory action projects such as examining "spatial location and demographic trends" in their community. Kinloch's most recent work demonstrated this kind of agency by inviting Harlem youth to "read" gentrification of their neighborhood (Kinloch, 2009c).

- Students can be ethnographers/anthropologists/sociolinguists and study the linguistic practices of others through close listening. Alim and Baugh (2007) do similar work with youth by asking them to study language in their homes and communities.

- Students can analyze the lyrics to their favorite songs and discuss linguistic patterns and then consider music in different regions of the country.

All these activities involve students in looking carefully at language use in real situations, a hands-on way to make *Students' Right to Their Own Language* come alive. Specifically, students become researchers who use writing to collect data and create final products.

We know that practices like these that develop students' literacy, numeracy, and technological, social, and political skills can help students become active participants in society (Ladson-Billings, 1995). As teachers who are responsible for the development of such skills, we are constantly searching for ways to prepare students for their futures as well as help them experience academic success, maintain cultural competence, and develop a critical consciousness—charges of culturally relevant pedagogy. Developing students' writing skills is one of the most demanding tasks for literacy teachers and is one that depends on constant assessment.

We are preparing them not only for standardized testing, but also for a life skill that they are most likely to need and use in any field of work, for any level of postsecondary educational endeavor, and in the workforce. Good assessment practices can help ensure that that happens. Culturally relevant assessment practices, approaches that help maintain students' investment in democratic classrooms, can further ensure that writing instruction and assessment do not become mundane activities met by student resistance. In the next few pages, we have collected a number of suggestions for ways teachers can continue to engage students in culturally relevant writing and ideas on how to link thoughtful assessment—both formal and informal—to those practices.

Include a wide range of texts for students to engage and make note of the texts they have chosen. Students should experience the work and words of people who share the same cultural background as well as those who are very different from them. Teachers can provide an array of writing examples from narratives, articles, lyrics, and poems, in which students experience characters who may look like them, authors who write about content students may empathize with or care about, and songs that they know and love. You can assess their progress in this area by making use of the aforementioned reading, writing, and thinking territories. As students record the titles and genres of the books they are reading or have read, they can respond as well to questions like these: "How will this book challenge me? What is new in this reading for me?" and "What culminating writing project (to be determined by teacher and student) best illuminates my new knowledge?" As you and your students look back at these records over time, not only do you have a way to note the number and kinds of books they've read, but you also can see what's changed, both in their approach to reading and in their ability to write.

Provide content for critique. Content and writing assignments can provide terrain for students to develop critical consciousness around issues of race, class, gender, and other social issues that affect their lives. Curriculum and practice should provide space for students to evaluate the world around them. Newspaper articles, editorials, and shows/movies that perpetuate stereotypes supply content for sparking critique around social issues. Again, teachers can do ongoing assessment of students' reactions to this content by asking open-ended questions, such as "What did you learn from reading this article?" or "How does this article connect to issues in your own life or community?"

Provide opportunities so that writing happens daily. Teachers should provide students the opportunity to write daily. Providing the space and time to write can serve many purposes. First, students have the opportunity to practice content and skills that can improve their writing, something that can be assessed on a regular basis. For example, when Latrise wanted to assess students' knowledge of a particular scene during the reading of a play or a chapter of a novel, she would pose several questions for students to choose from. And if she wanted to assess a particular skill they were working on at the same time, she would write a note on the board directing them to "pay attention to subject–verb agreement" or "watch verb tense" while they completed the writing. This daily practice and informal assessment of students' writing provided her with important information regarding where students were in terms of understanding the reading as well as what writing skills they still needed further instruction in.

Another way to invite daily writing and provide means for ongoing assessment is through journals. We have used journals in the beginning, middle, and at the end of lessons. Journals can be used to introduce topics, reinforce ideas, check for understanding, and provide students with a space to just write about things that may be on their minds. Below is a description of how different types of journals could be used in culturally relevant classrooms.

• *Life journals.* Latrise uses life journals at the beginning of the year both to preassess students' writing and to get to know students. Life journals rely on a series of questions that ask students about themselves. Students write about their lives, families, neighborhoods, likes/dislikes, hobbies, aspirations, and literate identities (in which they include their favorite books, magazines, video games, etc.). Students are also given the choice to include pictures, drawings, and other artifacts. Life journals can provide teachers with valuable information about students' individual identities as well as provide some insight into the type of content and texts students would enjoy.

• *Reader response journals.* Reader response journals invite students to answer questions related to the reading that takes place in class. A question (or a series of questions from which students can choose one) is usually posed by the teacher that reinforces ideas related to the text or is used to check comprehension. Earlier in this chapter, we mentioned that Latrise would have students respond to a question, but would also suggest that they pay attention to certain skills related to writing, usage, mechanics, and/or grammar. Coupling this practice with journal response can be used to reinforce skills that students need ongoing or extra practice with.

• *Character journals.* This idea entered Latrise's classroom while she was teaching one of her favorite books, *Seedfolks* by Paul Fleischman. To keep up with the actions, feelings, and important dialogue for each character, students developed a character journal in which they kept track of each character. Once Latrise and her students encountered a new character, they would record important information about that character. Latrise also encouraged students to create their own characters, which served as a kind of prewriting for one of the formal *Seedfolks* unit writing assignments, in which students created their own chapter for the novel that introduced a new character to the story line.

• *Place journals.* Like character journals, place journals can be a part of any reading. Place journals invite students to consider the settings of stories, including potential settings that students could include in their own writing. Students can also take place journals on school trips, personal vacations, or weekend outings. Having students keep place journals provides them opportunities to use their senses when describing settings and can increase the amount of detail they include in their writing.

Assessing the writing in these journals can take many forms: from recording how many pages students are writing, to noting how particular skills are being addressed, to seeing how journal entries connect to more formal pieces of writing.

Spark writing by encouraging dialogue. As we talked about in Chapter 4, having students discuss ideas and content not only gives students voice, but makes for a wonderful prewriting activity. Students and teachers share ideas, hear perspectives, and debate arguments that can add to the richness of their writing. Teachers can pose questions related to particular subject matter, current events, or themes arising from class readings. Engaging in dialogue can help students formulate ideas for their writing and can assist them in incorporating different perspectives and concrete examples. Dialogue is at the heart of writing in the culturally relevant classroom, yet it creates dilemmas for assessment: how do we capture spirited debates and dialogue and incorporate it into our assessment of student work? Because dialogue is a form of prewriting, we like the idea of teachers and students maintaining a dialogue chart in which student names in any given class period are already printed in table format with columns for teachers to record the intriguing ideas students raise in class discussion (see Figure 5.1). We also find this record helps with writing conferences; teachers can ask students to look back over the records in order to track their own development as active participants in classroom discussion.

Create/find writing assignments that are purposeful, meaningful, and/ or real. Writing can be frustrating for students, especially if they feel that they are writing just to write. It is important that teachers communicate

Figure 5.1. Classroom dialogue chart/teacher notes.

Student Names	Quote or illustration that I would like to remember	A clarifying question I would like to ask this student	Additional notes
Student A	"The only heroes for me are the ones I see every day...like my grandma and my mom..."	What are the examples of heroism in these women's daily lives?	Several students nodded in agreement to this quote and other hands were raised after this student spoke.
Student B	"I don't think we should consider any human being on earth to be a hero because it sets up false expectations. . . ."	Define "hero"? Can heroes be flawed?	Again, this quote inspired many other students to respond. . . . This student was asked by other students if his/her comment was based on religious views.

to students why writing is necessary for their lives (including academic success), the potential writing has to make meaning in their lives, and how and when writing is used in the "real world." Teachers can assign a purposeful writing activity that outlines a clear reason for writing, a role for the writer to assume, and an audience. Teachers can invite subject matter that connects to students' lives, just as Ms. Jane did when her students were encouraged to share their feelings on police brutality. Purposeful writing assignments in the culturally relevant classroom can include the following performance tasks:

- Letters to school administrators (principal, superintendent, school board) and the student body (skills: audience awareness, formatting, providing evidence, and using data).

- Letter to an editor of a relevant publication (skills: editing, revising, audience awareness).

- Position papers demonstrating both viewpoints so that students have to research various perspectives (skills: research, persuasive writing).

- Marketing presentations such as public service announcements and proposals for community projects (skills: media literacy, speech/scriptwriting).

- Conducting and compiling an anthology of interviews of members of the community (skills: oral communication, designing questions, organizing and synthesizing information).

Assessment of these can take many forms, but might include responses from the actual audience that the piece is intended for.

Create/find writing assignments that are creative (e.g., narratives, plays, poems, lyrics). Creative assignments often help students maintain a sense of cultural integrity by using their home language (e.g., African American Vernacular English, Spanglish), including creative vocabulary that comes from popular culture, or using content that connects to individual lives. While these kinds of assignments may seem more subjective and thus difficult to grade, teachers can assess word choice, sentence fluency, use of dialogue and dialogue mechanics, ideas, and organization. One way to assess a creative writing piece may be to consider the performance of such a text and how effective it is.

Model and share the processes and products of writing. Teachers provide great models for students. As a teacher, you can model the writing process by showing students what you do to actually write something, letting students hear how you are thinking about a piece of writing and how you expect to approach it. Teachers can also model writing products by supplying multiple examples of finished pieces, both exemplar pieces and those that are developing. Latrise, for example, usually writes with her students or brings personal samples for students to read and assess. Before getting started on their own writing, students have the opportunity to talk about ways examples could be improved or aspects of the piece that they could use in their own writing (see Figure 5.2). The example included here is one that Latrise used with preservice teachers to teach the concept of sharing the process of writing with students. This handout can, of course, be modified to fit other texts and writing processes. In this example, students read Cisneros's *The House on Mango Street* vignette, "My Name," and answer some questions related to the vignette. Then the teacher models for them how he or she would consider the writing task and asks students to provide feedback for his or her first draft.

Figure 5.2. Example of shared writing.

The House on Mango Street
Generating Ideas
"My Name" Vignette

Directions: Consider Esperanza's vignette "My Name" in order to write your own story about your name. In Esperanza's story we learn that her name means "hope" in English and, according to her, "too many letters . . . sadness . . . waiting" in Spanish. The following questions will guide you in creating ideas for your vignette.

1. What stories, if any, have family members or family friends told you about your name?
2. Are you named after anyone in your family? If so, who and what is he or she like?
3. What are the different translations/meanings of your name across cultures and languages? If your name is made up, give it a meaning.
4. What is your nickname? How did you get it?
5. Have you ever wanted to change your name, and if so, to what and why?
6. What else can you think about concerning your name?

Latrise's writing example of the assignment

My mom told me that my name should have been Michael or Maurice because my Dad wanted twin boys. Instead we were born girls and were named Latrise and Denise. My sister is Denise, the goddess of wine. Me, I am the goddess of nothing; my name was made-up. When I type my name, there is always a red line underneath it. The dictionary tells me that it should be "Latrine" which is a toilet. If I could choose, my name would mean angel, flower, or something delicate and fragile like statues made of sugar.

Modeling writing in the culturally relevant classroom does not simply stop at teachers sharing their work. Students should be provided space to have the agency to give teachers critical and specific written and verbal feedback on their work, identify vocabulary and concepts that are new, and ask questions. See Figure 5.3 (page 78) for an example of a feedback form that can be used for student-to-teacher, teacher-to-student, or student-to-student feedback.

We believe inviting students to comment on examples of writing, both good and not so good, both written by professionals and written by teachers, can help them identify issues that arise in their own writing. In a culturally relevant classroom, writing examples are often connected to their experiences and validate aspects of their lives. For example, the writing assignment above not only relates to *The House on Mango Street*, but it invites students to write about their own cultural and personal experiences as they relate to a piece of literature. In other words, a piece of writing that is exemplary and culturally relevant not only provides a model for writing, but becomes official content of a curriculum that is liberating and empowering for student writers.

The Small *a*: Informal Assessment of Students' Writing

One of the charges of culturally relevant writing instruction is that teachers provide instruction, content, and classroom practices that legitimize students' voices, knowledge, and experiences as official content of the class curriculum. And because assessment is an ingrained part of the writing instruction process, it requires that teachers take an ongoing look at students' writing to ensure they are developing skills they can use to articulate their ideas and experiences, cultivate their voices, and do both in a manner that empowers them to become skilled and confident writers. Alongside effective (and culturally relevant) writing instruction, we believe that the informal assessment of students' writing is a sure way to move their writing from good to great, from gold to platinum. While we briefly mentioned, in the previous section, some forms of informal and formal assessment in relation to specific strategies to teach writing, here we focus on some of our underlying beliefs about informal assessment, beliefs that not only support culturally relevant writing instruction but that offer teachers the kinds of information they can use to create a culture that will help all kids improve as writers.

Writing is assessed often and informally. Because writing is a complex process, routine assessments are needed. We do not mean that teachers should grade and/or comment on every piece of writing, nor do we mean that teachers should note every aspect to every piece of writing. However, generally knowing where students are in their progress as writers and what specific skills need further development can assist teachers in

Figure 5.3. Writing feedback form.

Name of the piece_____

Author _____

Person providing feedback _____

Writing Trait	Your comments
Ideas	What ideas do you consider to be good ones? What are ideas you would add?
Organization	How is the piece organized? What changes would you make?
Sentence fluency	Do the sentences flow well? Do sentences vary in beginning, length, and structure?
Word choice	What words do you find rich and descriptive? Which words would you replace?
Voice	Can you "hear" the author's voice in the piece? What seems to be the tone? If there doesn't seem to be a particular tone, what advice would you give?
Additional comments for the author	

planning classroom lessons and activities and improving student achievement. Because it is difficult to take on all aspects of writing at one time, students and teachers can keep track of daily writing so that students understand expectations for which traits and skills will be assessed at a given time. As we mentioned earlier, this might entail record keeping in which students and teachers focus on one or two qualities at a time (e.g., organization, voice, fluency, or specific conventions). To make this work, teachers must have a consistent record of the process, a chart that maps students' progress in those areas.

Because student prior knowledge is at the core of writing in the culturally relevant classroom, we also believe that in culturally relevant assessment, there should be an effort to assess more than product. Culturally relevant writing assessment must make note of the development of student ideas, the understanding of others' ideas, and how these two merge. For example, teachers can use discussion and questioning to get students thinking about content for their writing. The table structure in Figure 5.4 can be used to get students to begin generating ideas about a certain topic, something that can be modified to fit any unit of study. Over time, teachers can determine whether students make a shift from relying mostly on their own ideas to connecting their own ideas with those of others—both other authors whose work they've read and other students in their classroom.

Expectations for the finished product are provided upfront. As just mentioned, before students begin writing a piece that will be assessed, they should have the opportunity to discuss ideas and read related examples. In addition, students should be given a rubric or some kind of criteria that will be used to assess their writing. Giving students clear expectations for writing is a fair practice for the culturally relevant classroom so that students are not surprised or overwhelmed by all the intricacies of writing. A rubric can be used in several ways: not only to assess students' own

---

Figure 5.4. Assessing writing in the culturally relevant classroom: Growing ideas.

Developing Ideas around Police Brutality	Your ideas *(Personal experiences)*	Ideas generated from text *(Any media, including articles, TV, Internet)*	Ideas generated from discussion *(Testimonies of others)*
What positions/views are out there about police brutality?			
How does police brutality affect neighborhoods, communities, our nation, and the world?			

writing, but to assess the writing of other students, in magazine articles, and even of teacher models.

The rubrics given to students should be simple and readable. We like the scoring guides in Culham's (2003) *6+1 Traits of Writing*, in which the traits of writing (ideas, sentence fluency, organization, word choice, voice, and conventions) can be assessed separately or all at once. A teacher, for example, may choose to focus any given assignment on organization or word choice or a grammar-related issue, such as the correct usage of *your* and *you're* or *its* and *it's*. Foci can be classwide or can be based in the needs of individual students. For example, students who require spelling practice but not subject–verb agreement practice should not have to sit through mini-lessons or complete assignments related to subject–verb agreement. Students and teachers can focus instead on areas where students need support so that their writing can continue to move toward platinum status.

Using rubrics or some kind of informal record of particular areas of emphasis over the course of the semester can provide you with details on how individual students are progressing. For example, you may note in your daily assessment that a student may need to pay further attention to word choice or developing details, a specific skill that might be quite different from the skills that others in the class need to work on. While there are many writing rubrics that can be used, we also encourage teachers to create their own informal record that allows for the categories that make sense, perhaps even a category for assessing the development of ideas as well as students' abilities to support new ideas.

Students have the opportunity to self-assess. Writing in the culturally relevant classroom encourages students to have ownership of their process and products; therefore, students should have ownership over the assessment process as well. Teachers can help students become more skilled in doing this by creating meaningful self-assessments. NCTE and IRA's ReadWriteThink website is one resource that offers sound ideas about self-assessment; among their suggestions for self-assessment strategies in practice are these:

> • Student can participate in creating rubrics for their writing assignments.

> • Students and teachers can co-create learning contracts identifying learning objectives and outcomes.

> • Students should have access to a space for "muddy points" or outstanding issues, questions, and topics they would like to revisit.

> • Students can be invited to share their work anonymously for public feedback.

> • Students can write letters to or present to future students what they have learned and what these students can expect in their

classes (we especially like the idea of seniors presenting to juniors, juniors presenting to sophomores, etc. at the end of the academic year [adapted from Wilder, 2011]).

Students are provided spaces to share their writing. Even the shortest pieces of writing can be displayed in the classroom. Student writing should adorn classroom walls and bulletin boards, as well as be displayed on classroom blogs and publications. Students can also be encouraged to publish outside of the classroom (e.g., school newspapers, community newsletters, school website, poetry/prose readings, school programs) as well as to regularly exchange their work with other students in the classroom. When students know that they will share their work with others, they are more likely to put forth greater effort to make their writing audience ready. While sharing writing with others is a mainstay of good writing practice, sharing writing in the culturally relevant classroom takes on an added dimension: to create a more democratic setting, students can work with teachers to manage the means and locations of that sharing. Students should have bulletin space they manage and learn to look at their work together in order to achieve distributive ownership of the classroom. Maisha's work with Poppa Joe and the Power Writers demonstrated, for example, how students and teachers could engage in a "read and feed process" (Fisher, 2005a, 2005b, 2007; Winn & Ubiles, 2011). In this process, students and teachers read original work and receive feedback from two students (who are selected ahead of time). The Power Writers held public readings at least once a semester and participated in local events including the Brave New Voices youth poetry competition drawing from youth poets and writers from cities throughout the United States and abroad.

Writing conferences take place regularly. Scheduled writing conferences are integral to any writing course. During this one-on-one time with the teacher, students can ask questions about their writing, get clarification on comments teachers may have made, and receive extra help on particular skills or content. To make this process go as smoothly as possible, Latrise often made a chart about each student's piece of writing with anecdotal notes about the writing on the left side of the template, student concerns on the right side, and next steps for the writer on the bottom (see Figure 5.5).

Teacher feedback is clear and concise. Whether teachers are providing feedback during a conference or on students' papers, they should write comments and/or suggestions that are clear and concise. Be specific. Let students know why something is "good." For example, you might want to say, "This is a good sentence because you chose some very colorful and concrete words to describe your dream." It's also important to include how a statement may have been unclear, such as, "This sentence is a little confusing to me because I don't see how it relates to other sentences in the paragraph." Using specifics in this way may help students develop

Figure 5.5. Anecdotal notes about student writing.

Name of the piece_____

Author _____

Person providing feedback _____

Teacher Comments	Writer's Concerns

Writer's Next Steps

more "good" writing and prevent them from repeating the same errors again and again.

A variety of writing is assessed. Though students may have to take state assessments that assess their essay writing, it may also be helpful to consider other types of writing to assess as well. It is important to assess multiple genres of writing so that students can recognize their various strengths that may be apparent in particular genres. Teachers can build students' capacities to write by starting small, and increasing length and skill as instruction progresses and as students master skills.

The Big *A*: Formal Assessment of Student Writing

With any subject, there has to be an evaluation in which students' mastery of skills and/or content is formally assessed. We think of formal assessment as a way to assign a number or grade related to a certain level of mastery. According to the Common Core State Standards Initiative:

> Each year in their writing, students should demonstrate increasing sophistication in all aspects of language use, from vocabulary and syntax to the development and organization of ideas, and they should address increasingly demanding content and sources. Students advancing through the grades are expected to meet each year's grade-specific standards and retain or further develop skills and understandings mastered in preceding grades. (2010)

Although there is no one number that could indicate a student's mastery of certain writing skills, teachers must have some way of knowing the writing capacities of students, which skills and/or genres are students' strongest, and at what levels students' writing meets or does not meet standards. While informal or formative assessments provide us with some information, we believe there is a place for formal assessment, too. Why is this important in a culturally relevant classroom? Because writers are often judged by the final pieces they produce—in standardized tests, in the writing they submit in college, in the writing they do at their place of work. It is our job, then, to help prepare all kids for that kind of assessment, too. How can we conduct formal assessment in a way that supports the ideals of a culturally relevant approach to writing instruction?

Although rubrics were discussed earlier, we feel it useful to revisit the idea here because they are key to affixing a specific number that represents a certain level of writing competency. Most state writing exams are assessed using a rubric similar to the one referred to previously, in which particular traits of writing are assessed apart from others (e.g., content, organization, style, grammar, and mechanics). To create a fair playing field, all students should have the opportunity to become familiar with the language of these high-stakes rubrics. Part of the teacher's role, then, is to offer class time to talk about the vocabulary of the rubrics, to immerse students in the way rubrics work, and to look carefully at sample writing that has been scored according to rubrics.

Formal assessment of writing is not limited to essays (although it is equally important to include them), which are commonly seen as a part of state and national writing assessments. In the following sections, we discuss several ways to formally assess a variety of students' writing, approaches that incorporate culturally relevant pedagogic ideas, and ways to effectively assess students' skills and development.

Portfolios

Assigning portfolios to formally assess students' writing is a way of assessing numerous writing pieces completed by students. For a ninth-grade literature unit Latrise taught on *Tangerine* by Edward Bloor, for example, students were asked to complete numerous writing assignments for the unit: reader responses to particular entries (the book is arranged with dated entries written in first person by the protagonist); character journals; a list of images and symbols, along with their meanings; and an essay that responded to the prompt, "Should families keep secrets? Consider the secret that was kept from Paul by his family. Do you think it is best to keep secrets from family members or should families always tell the truth? Explain your position and provide examples from the novel and ones that you may have experienced." For the portfolio, students were invited to choose three reader responses, three entries from their character journals, five symbols and their meanings, and the essay. Participating in a portfolio-based classroom gives students both the opportunity to revise writing that they may want to include and a chance to choose what they think is their best writing. Students are assessed on their most polished writing because they have a chance to practice particular genres. They also collect ideas along the way as they experience texts, get feedback, and engage discussions. With this form of assessment, students' writing is formally assessed in a way that ensures academic success due to careful and deliberate writing instruction and informal assessment that were concerned with improving the skills of student writers along the way.

Digital Portfolios

If teachers have the necessary technology, digital portfolios can be fun for students. A digital portfolio is a lot like any portfolio in that it is a collection of students' writing. However, digital portfolios can work in several ways. First, students use technology tools for publishing their portfolios. Students may keep electronic journals (in a word document or blog) and create electronic versions of required assignments. Another way to consider digital portfolios is as a living document. Instead of printing or saving portfolios, students can create webpages that include hyperlinks to their work, or they could do the same with blogging. When publishing digital portfolios, students should understand that certain standards are to be met before they send their work out into the world. Again, the processes by which this happens ensure a level of writing that will meet or exceed standards because students' writing classroom experiences calls for this.

Multiple Genres

We realize that with the increased emphasis on standardized testing and common standards, certain genres of writing take center stage. Teachers, concerned that students' performances on short essay exams will be used to assess students' overall writing ability (and, at times, their teaching ability), necessarily emphasize that genre in the classroom. However, we believe that in order for students to be successful writers beyond school, they need exposure to multiple genres, and that assessing these genres can offer us great insight into students' abilities.

Plays (Stage/Screenplays)

Why have students write plays? Writing a play is a great cooperative writing activity that can assist students with creating characters and writing dialogue. Also, it provides an exciting way for them to share their writing (by acting). Having students write an entire original play may be an optimistic undertaking. However, students can write short scenes or acts instead. For example, in her tenth-grade literature class, Latrise asked students to rewrite Alice Walker's "Everyday Use." Students worked in cooperative learning groups to create dialogue and scene notes that were based on the short story. Assessing student work in this case offered insights into their understanding of the short story, their skills in creating dialogue, and their ability to work in groups. While assessing this kind of cooperative writing can be tough, it is important that students work together to produce writing as this models the kind of real-life situations they'll be part of in the future. Why assess playwriting? The critical feedback and assessment of cooperative writing assignments may provide particular students with a less intimidating evaluation of their work. In addition, a student could be particularly strong in dialogue writing, something that might not show up in assessment of other types of writing. To assess students' cooperative writing activities, specific tasks can be assigned to each individual student, which you may use to assign individual grades, if assigning grades is of major concern.

Essay Writing

Essay writing is very important to a student's academic career. In most cases, students are assessed, by many states, at least three times during their matricula-tion. Assessing essay writing can be overwhelming because there are many aspects that make a good essay (e.g., the six traits of writing). However, we think that it is helpful to consider one or two traits at a time and, since conventions refer to many skills, that teachers only focus on a few at a time. We also think it is important to note that teachers can assign an essay prompt, use writers workshop to teach a mini-lesson related to a particular trait, assess the piece of writing, then begin again with the same essay but a different trait. This process can teach what one of our most esteemed colleagues, Vanessa Siddle-Walker, would call the "art of revision."

Revisiting NCTE Belief Statements about Writing

Each of NCTE's belief statements about writing suggests the importance of cul-turally relevant pedagogy, especially the three statements that we referred to at the start of this book. First, according to NCTE, "Everyone has the capacity to write, writing can be taught, and teachers can help students become better writers." Em-bedded in this statement is the notion that literacy is a "civil right" (Green, 2010) and that all students, regardless of race, class, gender, level of exposure, or academ-ic level, deserve access to writing instruction. The languages and literacies students already possess give them the capacity to become effective writers. Aforementioned writing instruction and assessment that considers culturally relevant pedagogy and content welcomes the voices and perspectives of students without upholding a standard form of literacy. Instead, students engage multiple literacies and are urged to meet all those literacies with high expectations.

In addition, *NCTE Beliefs about the Teaching of Writing* suggest that "[w]riting grows out of many different purposes." Having students experience multiple writ-ing assessments creates opportunities for students to engage the types of writing they will encounter in the world. And most significantly, perhaps, is the belief that "Literate practices are embedded in complicated social relationships." One of the most important aspects of culturally relevant pedagogy is that of building a community of writers who have a forum to share and discuss their ideas with each other.

Conclusion

Teachers who are looking for ways to allow culturally relevant pedagogy to take shape in their classrooms can use the aforementioned instruction and assessment practices. Inviting writing assessment that allows for a broad definition of literacy to rip the seams of traditional views of literacy incorporates the reading, writing, speaking, and performance practices that are customary in the lives of youth. Writing is a natural fit for pairing culturally relevant pedagogy in order to create meaningful learning opportunities for all students. Though teachers must be strategic and deliberate in the ways in which they consider content, curriculum, and culturally relevant pedagogy right alongside writing instruction and assessment, doing so can have a positive effect on the educational outcomes for students in our classrooms.

Providing students with numerous opportunities to write for different purposes and audiences while accounting for lived and cultural experiences are key aspects of a culturally relevant writing classroom. As literacy teachers, we are charged with providing students with the reading and writing skills that will help them pass standardized tests as well as communicate effectively in college and in life. Teachers can confront issues of cultural differences in language and writing structures by (1) inviting a variety of writing structures into the writing classroom, (2) explicitly teaching purpose and audience, (3) providing well-written, culturally relevant texts as models, (4) assessing the process of writing, and (5) inviting students to contend with personal and cultural issues within their writing. Writing in a culturally relevant classroom does not mean that we do away with standards. However, it does require us to acknowledge differences and create spaces in which students can celebrate, confront, and contend with those differences. Writing is a natural fit for such celebrating, confronting, and contending and we believe that there is an immediate need to do so within literacy classrooms in order to take students' writing from gold to platinum.

Annotated Bibliography: Latrise and Maisha's Infinite Playlist

Below are some of the books, short stories, anthologies, music, and poetry that Maisha and Latrise have found to have cultural relevance for students in their classrooms. Included in the list are books that we have encountered over the past years as we worked with middle and high school students and preservice teachers. We also offer suggestions for writing instruction, assignments/tasks, and assessments that could happen as a result of engaging each work.

Achebe, Chinua
Things Fall Apart
New York: Anchor Books, 1994

Once again, hip-hop comes to the rescue! The Roots, hip-hop's primary example of musicianship, named one of their celebrated albums *Things Fall Apart*. Each track, referred to as chapters that continue from previous recordings, offers a journey through The Roots' musical experiences. We ask students to write about why this group would employ the title of Achebe's famous novel in their album. In Latrise's class, students were divided into tribes and had to write about fabricated issues that would arise within and between their fictitious tribes. Today, we would like to see Achebe's novel discussed against the backdrop of a talk given by another Nigerian writer, Chimimanda Adichie. Adichie's talk, "The Danger of a Single Story," warns against the ways in which ignorance and misperceptions can deter people from learning how dynamic and multidimensional people are in this world. Students can view Adichie's talk (available on TED: http://www.ted.com/talks/lang/eng/chimamanda_adichie_the_danger_of_a_single_story.html) and write a response to the "single story" that has stopped people from learning their true identity and intentions.

Allende, Isabel
The House of the Spirits
New York: Knopf, 1982

The possibilities are endless! Part of Maisha's approach to Allende's *The House of Spirits* is inviting students to keep a *House of Spirits* journal including critical reading reflections for each chapter. A tenth-grade world literature class took this project and ran with it; students created handmade journals, portraits of all the *House of Spirits* characters (all of these had to be accompanied by a piece of writing), poems for each chapter, and the best thing was no student was willing to let Maisha keep his or her project to use as a future example. They wanted to keep them all!

Bloor, Edward
Tangerine
San Diego: Harcourt Brace, 1997

Another great boy book! This story is about a visually impaired boy in middle school who discovers a dark family secret. This story has suspense and uses imagery and symbols. Students can discuss and write about diversity, disability, and the sense of belonging. Teachers can use this book to teach literary elements, including characterization. The book lends itself to numerous writing activities and prompts that deal with a variety of subject matter that students can connect to their own lives. For example, students can write about issues around puberty, sibling rivalry, and physical impairments.

Cisneros, Sandra
The House on Mango Street
New York: Knopf, 1994

We cannot say enough about *The House on Mango Street*! This was the first book that many of Maisha's tenth-grade literature students completed cover to cover. On some editions there is an endorsement from the legendary Chicago poet Gwendolyn Brooks. Brooks's and Cisneros's work can be used together to illuminate issues that have plagued both black and Latino communities. We talk about many of these ideas in Chapters 3 and 4.

Creech, Sharon
Love That Dog
New York: HarperCollins, 2001

Set up as journal entries from a student, this novel reveals a growing understanding of poetry as Jack learns to read and write poems through imaginative lessons from his teacher. Jack is especially inspired by a poem by Walter Dean Myers titled "Love That Boy," which is an ode to his son. A great book to teach alongside this is *Blues Journey* by Walter Dean Myers with illustrations by his son Christopher Myers. That extended poem has many poetic elements that teachers can share with students, and it deals with the trying moments that affect individuals' lives. Latrise has used these books during poetry units with eighth and ninth graders. *Love That Dog* is a short read and is a good book to use with readers of any level. *Blues Journey* is a wonderful book to share aloud and discuss the ideas tangled in African American culture along the way. Students can keep journals about their engagement with poetry or can write poetry of their own.

Def Poetry Jam/HBO Original Series
Perhaps no other show has skillfully brought together the new generation of poets, artists, and writers with the women and men who shaped the poetry of the Black Arts movement. In addition to featuring poets throughout the country, Def Poetry Jam always celebrates the work of a foremother or forefather in poetry. From Sonia Sanchez, Nikki Giovanni, and Felipe Luciano to Amiri Baraka and Haki Madhubuti, Def Poetry is a work of art.

Dickinson, Emily
"My life had stood – a loaded gun"
Shakur, Tupac
"Me and my girlfriend"
When given several writing options, many of Maisha's students chose to create a dialogue between Dickinson's poem and Shakur's rap song; their poetry and lyrics have been brought together in wonderful collections and recordings. Students could write comparative essays that provide an analysis of the similarities and differences of the poem and rap. Please note that some of Shakur's lyrics are explicit and should be used with discretion.

Fleischman, Paul
Seedfolks
New York: HarperCollins, 1997

A good read for raising one's social consciousness. Because the story is told from many perspectives, readers get to experience prejudice from different ethnic and national groups. Latrise used this book in her eighth-grade class in which students discussed, researched, and wrote about issues around immigration, American culture, and nature. Also, at the end, students included their own chapter of *Seedfolks* and were assessed on characterization and voice.

Grimes, Nikki
Bronx Masquerade
New York: Dial Books, 2002

Like *Seedfolks*, *Bronx Masquerade* is a story told from multiple perspectives about a middle school class that is experiencing poetry as a result of studying the Harlem Renaissance. As a result of the unit, their teacher provides space every Friday for them to share their poetry during open mic. This book is easy to read and could inspire content for students' poetry as the book deals with issues that matter to middle-school-aged kids. Other than inspiration for poetry, the book could be used alongside character journals.

McBride, James
The Color of Water: A Black Man's Tribute to His White Mother
New York: Penguin Books, 1996

McBride's memoir of growing up biracial with his Jewish mother was a *New York Times* bestseller for years. McBride's rich and powerful language conveys a sense of yearning and desire to belong, along with great warmth and admiration for his mother. One of the interesting issues in the book is how young McBride and his siblings were experiencing the Black Power Movement and an increasing awareness of their blackness. When using this text with preservice teachers, we realized that many were unaware of the particulars of the Black Power Movement (we highly recommend reading the work of Peniel E. Joseph for some of the most compelling analysis of this important movement). In one of our learning stations, we provide a copy of the Black Panther Party Platform along with a recording of one of its celebrated leaders, Bobby Seale, reading it publicly. This experience has always been illuminating for teachers because while they have learned about the Civil Rights Movement, they have too often learned to marginalize the Black Power and Black Arts Movements. We also invite students to create a "platform" for McBride's mother, Ruthie, who has very clear expectations of her children; these platforms must demonstrate knowledge of the text.

Morrison, Toni
Beloved
New York: Penguin Books, 1987

When Maisha first read *Beloved* in an eleventh-grade American literature class, she was dazed and confused. Even after reading it in an undergraduate class, she still did not "get it." However, during graduate school Maisha gave it one more chance in a seminar entitled "Images of African American Women in Literature" taught by Barbara Christian. Professor Christian's seminar was transformative. Christian placed Morrison and *Beloved* in a historical context that made sense and did not ignore the obvious—to teach *Beloved*, you must talk about the horrors of the enslavement of Africans in the Americas. To omit slavery from any discussion of this text is to do students a disservice. Maisha was able to return to her former high school and participate in helping eleventh graders "get" *Beloved*. Maisha opened her lesson by displaying a quilt made of fabric from different dresses (the same idea can be achieved using a necktie quilt or anything with an unexpected pattern) to discuss how the story of *Beloved* comes together out of many stories. The other key piece in teaching *Beloved* is the focus on what Morrison had to do as a writer—conduct research and study the contraptions used on slaves to keep them quiet (the bit) and in line (the coffle). There are many opportunities to bring history and social studies into the teaching of this rich novel.

Morrison, Toni
The Bluest Eye
New York: Vintage Books, 1970

While leading an after school book club, Maisha introduced Morrison's *The Bluest Eye* through the hip-hop group Black Star (comprising rappers Mos Def and Talib Kweli). On their self-entitled album, the rappers include extensive liner notes about their experiences writing each song and what inspired the work. The last track, "Thieves in the Night," is an ode to Toni Morrison and other black writers who Kweli refers to as "preservers of Black culture." It is wonderful to have students juxtapose Black Star's lyrics with Morrison's text. Using these two texts can also serve as a foundation to discuss intertextuality. Maisha would never teach this book without including Black Star's song, lyrics, and inspiration. Latrise also taught this book and used the events around the life of Pecola, the protagonist of the novel, to discuss ideas around identity, loss, family, tragedy, and delusion.

Myers, Walter Dean
Monster
New York: HarperCollins, 1999

This is a great boy book. It begins as a movie

script and reveals to the reader the American legal system through the eyes of a 16-year-old African American male on trial for murder. It is a good book to teach plot and dialogue, and it is great for students to read aloud. It can also spark dialogue around stereotypes of African American males and issues of justice. Students can write their own movie scripts about an event in their own lives or create opening and closing arguments that they draft and share in a classroom courtroom.

Neruda, Pablo
Odes to Common Things
New York: Little, Brown, 1994

What better way to get students to engage poetry and write some of their own than assigning writing odes to their "common things"? Neruda is masterful and we (and our students) love his subtlety. Also, if you have time, you should consider adding the film *il Postino*, which explores Neruda's life and celebrates the metaphor. Students could write their own odes and could produce short films related to their odes.

Walker, Alice
"Everyday Use." In In Love and Trouble: Stories of Black Women
New York: Harcourt Brace Jovanovich, 1974

One of Latrise's favorite short stories to teach is Alice Walker's "Everyday Use." This story examines whether heritage should be preserved or integrated in one's daily life. Latrise's students wrote persuasive letters to Mama either encouraging her to send Dee the quilts for the preservation of a rich history or urging her to stay with her decision to put the quilts to everyday use. Students also turned this short story into a stage play by creating dialogue for each of the characters.

Works Cited

Adichie, C. (2009). *Chimamanda Adichie: The danger of a single story* [Video]. Retrieved from http://www.ted.com/talks/chimamanda_adichie_the_danger_of_a_single_story.html

Alim, H. S., & Baugh, J. (Eds.). (2007). *Talkin black talk: Language, education, and social change*. New York: Teachers College Press.

Ancess, J. (2008). Small alone is not enough. *Educational Leadership, 65*(8), 48–53.

Atwell, N. (1998). *In the middle: New understandings about writing, reading, and learning* (2nd ed.). Portsmouth, NH: Boynton/Cook.

Banks, J. A. (2007). *Educating citizens in a multicultural society* (2nd ed.). New York: Teachers College Press.

Berliner, D. C. (1989). Implications of studies of expertise in pedagogy for teacher education and evaluation. In J. Pfleiderer (Ed.), *New directions for teacher assessment: Proceedings of the 1988 ETS invitational conference* (pp. 39–67). Princeton, NJ: Educational Testing Service.

Boyd, F. B., & Brock, C. H. (with Rozendal, M. S.). (Eds.). (2004). *Multicultural and multilingual literacy and language: Contexts and practices*. New York: Guilford Press.

Branch, J. P. (Director/Producer/Writer). (2005). *Under the radar: A survey of Afro-Cuban music* [DVD].

Brooks, G. (1945). *A street in Bronzeville*. New York: Harper.

Brooks, G., & Ringgold, F. (1956/2007). *Bronzeville boys and girls*. New York: Amistad/HarperCollins.

Christensen, L. (2000). *Reading, writing, and rising up. Teaching about social justice and the power of the written word*. Milwaukee, WI: Rethinking Schools.

Cisneros, S. (1984). *The house on Mango Street*. New York: Vintage Books.

Cofer, J. O. (1995). *An island like you: Stories of the barrio*. New York: Orchard Books.

Common Core State Standards Initiative. (2010). *Common core state standards for English language arts and literacy in history/social studies, science, and technical subjects*. Retrieved from http://www.corestandards.org/assets/CCSSI_ELA%20Standards.pdf

Conference on College Composition and Communication of the National Council of Teachers of English. (1974). *Students' right to their own language*. Retrieved from http://www.ncte.org/library/NCTEFiles/Groups/CCCC/NewSRTOL.pdf

Cox, M., Ortmeier-Hooper, C., & Tirabassi, K. E. (2009). Teaching writing for the "real world": Community and workplace writing. *English Journal, 98*(5), 72–80.

Creech, S. (2001). *Love that dog*. New York: HarperCollins.

Culham, R. (2003). *6+1 traits of writing: The complete guide, grades 3 and up*. New York: Scholastic.

Delpit, L. (1996). *Other people's children: Cultural conflict in the classroom*. New York: New Press.

Diallo, K. (2004). *My heart will cross this ocean: My story, my son, Amadou*. New York: One World-Ballantine Books.

Duncan, G. A. (2000). Urban pedagogies and the celling of adolescents of color. *Social Justice, 27*(3) 29–42.

Dyson, A. H. (2005). Crafting "The humble prose of living": Rethinking oral/written relations in the echoes of spoken word. *English Education, 37,* 149–164.

Fecho, B. (2004). *"Is this English?" Race, language, and culture in the classroom*. New York: Teachers College Press.

Ferguson, M., Salter, M. J., & Stallworthy, J. (Eds.). (2005). *The Norton anthology of poetry* (5th ed.). New York: Norton.

Fisher, M. T. (2003). Open mics and open minds: Spoken word poetry in African diaspora participatory literacy communities. *Harvard Educational Review, 73,* 362–389.

Fisher, M. T. (2004). "The song is unfinished": The new literate and literary and their institutions. *Written Communication, 21,* 290–312.

Fisher, M. T. (2005a). From the coffee house to the school house: The promise and potential of spoken word poetry in school contexts. *English Education, 37,* 115–131.

Fisher, M. T. (2005b). *Literocracy*: Liberating language and creating possibilities: An introduction. *English Education, 37,* 92–95.

Fisher, M. T. (2007). *Writing in rhythm: Spoken word poetry in urban classrooms*. New York: Teachers College Press.

Fisher, M. T. (2008). Catching butterflies. *English Education, 40,* 94–100.

Fisher, M. T. (2009). *Black literate lives: Historical and contemporary perspectives*. New York: Routledge.

Fisher, M. T., Spear Purcell, S., & May, R. (2009). Process, product, and playmaking. *English Education, 41,* 337–355.

Fishman, J., Lunsford, A., McGregor, B., & Otuteye, M. (2005). Performing writing, performing literacy. *College Composition and Communication, 57,* 224–252.

Fox, M., & Fine, M. (in press). Circulating critical research: Reflections on performance and moving inquiry into action. In G. Cannella & S. Steinberg (Eds.), *Critical qualitative research reader*. New York: Peter Lang.

Gadsden, V. L., & Wagner, D. A. (Eds.). (1995). *Literacy among African American youth: Issues in learning, teaching, and schooling*. Cresskill, NJ: Hampton Press.

Gay, G. (2000). *Culturally responsive teaching: Theory, research, and practice*. New York: Teachers College Press.

Georgia Department of Education. (2006). Georgia performance standard - ELA10W1. Retrieved from https://www.georgiastandards.org/_layouts/GeorgiaStandards/Unitbuilder/SearchResults.aspx?viewmode=details&StandardIDSelected=393

Giroux, H. A., & Simon, R. I. (1989). *Popular culture, schooling, and everyday life*. New York: Bergin and Garvey.

González, N. E., Moll, L., & Amanti, C. (2005). *Funds of knowledge: Theorizing practices in households, communities, and classrooms*. Mahwah, NJ: Erlbaum.

Green, K. (2010). *Youth speaking truth: The literacy practices of a youth-centered radio program*. Unpublished manuscript, Emory University, Atlanta, GA.

Grimes, N. (2002). *Bronx masquerade*. New York: Penguin.

Gutiérrez, K. D., & Vossoughi, S. (2010). Lifting off the ground to return anew: Mediated praxis, transformative learning, and social design experiments. *Journal of Teacher Education, 61*, 100–117.

Hill, L. (1998). *The miseducation of Lauryn Hill* [CD]. New York: Sony.

Hill, M. L. (2009). *Beats, rhymes, and classroom life: Hip-hop pedagogy and the politics of identity*. New York: Teachers College Press.

Hudson, W. (2004). *Powerful words: More than 200 years of extraordinary writing by African Americans*. New York: Scholastic.

Hughes, L. (1990). *Selected poems of Langston Hughes*. New York: Vintage.

Irvine, J. J. (1991). *Black students and school failure: Policies, practices, and prescriptions*. New York: Praeger.

Irvine, J. J. (1992). Making teacher education culturally responsive. In M. E. Dilworth (Ed.), *Diversity in teacher education: New expectations* (pp. 79–92). San Fransisco: Jossey-Bass.

Irvine, J. J. (Ed.). (2002). *In search of wholeness: African American teachers and their culturally specific classroom practices*. New York: Palgrave.

Irvine, J. J. (2003). *Educating teachers for diversity: Seeing with a cultural eye*. New York: Teachers College Press.

Jocson, K. M. (2008). *Youth poets: Empowering literacies in and out of schools*. New York: Peter Lang.

Johnson, L. P. (2010). *Re-defining a literate identity: African American male youth, literacy, and schooling*. Unpublished empirical study, Emory University, Atlanta, Georgia.

Johnson, T. H. (Ed.). (1961). *Final harvest: Emily Dickenson's poems*. Boston: Little, Brown.

Jordan, J., & Muller, L. (Eds.). (1995). *June Jordan's poetry for the people: A revolutionary blueprint*. New York: Routledge.

Karunuñgan, M. L. L. (2002). Chasing hope through culturally relevant praxis: One master teacher and her African American eighth grade readers. In J. J. Irvine (Ed.), *In search of wholeness: African American teachers and their culturally specific classroom practices* (pp.113–137). New York: Palgrave.

Khan, E. (2009). Making writing instruction authentic. *English Journal, 98*(5), 15–17.

Kinloch, V. (2005) Revisiting the promise of *Students' right to their own language*: Pedagogical strategies. *College Composition and Communication, 57*, 83–113.

Kinloch, V. (2009a). Literacy, community, and youth acts of place-making. *English Education, 41*, 316–336.

Kinloch, V. (2009b). Power, politics, and pedagogies: Re-imagining students' right to their own language through democratic engagement. In J. C. Cobb, D. Y. Straker, & L. Katz, (Eds.), *Affirming students' right to their own language: Bridging language policies and pedagogical practices* (pp. 85–98). New York: Routledge; Urbana, IL: National Council of Teachers of English.

Kinloch, V. (2009c). Suspicious special distinctions: Literacy research with students across school and community contexts. *Written Communication, 26*, 154–182.

Kinloch, V. (2010). *Harlem on our minds: Place, race, and the literacies of urban youth*. New York: Teachers College Press.

Kirkland, D. E. (2007). The power of their texts: Using hip hop to help urban students meet NCTE/IRA national standards for the English language arts. In K. K. Jackson & S. Vavra (Eds.), *Closing the gap: English educators address the tensions between teacher preparation and teaching writing in secondary schools* (pp.129–145). Charlotte, NC: Information Age.

Kirkland, D. E. (2009). The skin we ink: Tattoos, literacy, and a new English education. *English Education, 41*, 375–395.

Ladson-Billings, G. (1992). Liberatory consequences of literacy: A case of culturally relevant instruction for African American students. *Journal of Negro Education, 61*, 378–391.

Ladson-Billings, G. (1994). *The dreamkeepers: Successful teachers of African American children*. San Francisco: Jossey-Bass.

Ladson-Billings, G. (1995). But that's just good teaching! The case for culturally relevant pedagogy. *Theory into Practice, 34*, 159–165.

Ladson-Billings, G. (2006). From the achievement gap to the education debt: Understanding achievement in U.S. schools. *Educational Researcher, 35*, 3–12.

Lee, C. D. (2000). Signifying in the zone of proximal development. In C. D. Lee & P. Smagorinsky (Eds.), *Vygotskian perspectives on literacy research: Constructing meaning through collaborative inquiry* (pp.191–225). New York: Cambridge University Press.

Lee, C. D. (2007). *Culture, literacy, and learning: Blooming in the midst of the whirlwind*. New York: Teachers College Press.

Lee, J., Grigg, W., & Donahue, P. (2007). *The nation's report card: Reading 2007* (NCES 2007–496). Washington, DC: National Center for Education Statistics, Institute of Education Sciences, U.S. Department of Education. Retrieved from http://nces.ed.gov/pubsearch/pubsinfo.asp?pubid=2007496

Lipman, P. (2008). Education policy, race, and neoliberal urbanism. In S. Greene (Ed.), *Literacy as a civil right: Reclaiming social justice in literacy teaching and learning* (pp. 45–68). New York: Peter Lang.

Madsen, J. A., & Mabokela, R. O. (2005). *Culturally relevant schools: Creating positive workplace relationships and preventing intergroup differences*. New York: Routledge.

Mahiri, J. (1998). *Shooting for excellence: African American youth culture in new century schools*. Urbana, IL: National Council of Teachers of English; New York: Teachers College Press.

Mahiri, J. (Ed.). (2004). *What they don't learn in school: Literacy in the lives of urban youth*. New York: Peter Lang.

Marable, M. (2006). *Living black history: How reimagining the African-American past can remake America's racial future*. New York: Basic Civitas Books.

McHenry, E., & Heath, S. B. (1994). The literate and the literary: African Americans as writers and readers, 1830–1940. *Written Communication, 11*, 419–444.

McKibbin, K. (2005). *Project Notes: Conducting oral history in the secondary classroom*. New York: Student Press Initiative.

Meiners, E. R. (2007). *Right to be hostile: Schools, prisons, and the making of public enemies*. New York: Routledge.

Michie, G. (1999). *Holler if you hear me: The education of a teacher and his students*. New York: Teachers College Press.

Moore-Hart, M. A. (2005). A writers' camp in action: A community of readers and writers. *The Reading Teacher, 59(4)*, 326–338.

Morrell, E. (2008). *Critical literacy and urban youth: Pedagogies of access, dissent, and liberation*. New York: Routledge.

Morrison, T. (1987). *Beloved*. New York: Knopf.

Morrison, T. (2000). *The bluest eye*. New York: Random House. (Original work published 1970).

Myers, W. D. (2003). *Blues journey*. New York: Holiday House.

National Council of Teachers of English, Writing Study Group of the NCTE Executive Committee. (2004). *NCTE Beliefs about the teaching of writing.* Retrieved from http://www.ncte.org/positions/statements/writingbeliefs

Neruda, P. (1994). *Odes to common things* (K. Krabbenhoft, Trans.). Boston: Little, Brown.

Nieto, S. (1999). *The light in their eyes: Creating multicultural learning communities.* New York: Teachers College Press.

Nieto, S. (2000). *Affirming diversity: The sociopolitical context of multicultural education* (3rd ed.). New York: Longman.

Nieto, S. (2003). *What keeps teachers going?* New York: Teachers College Press.

Noguera, P. A. (2008). *The trouble with black boys and other reflections on race, equity, and the future of public education.* San Francisco: Jossey Bass.

Obidah, J. E. (1998). Black-mystory: Literate currency in everyday schooling. In D. E. Alvermann, K. A. Hinchman, D. W. Moore, S. F. Phelps, & D. R. Waff (Eds.), *Reconceptualizing the literacies in adolescents' lives* (pp. 51–71). Mahwah, NJ: Erlbaum.

Ogbu, J. U. (1981). School ethnography: A multilevel approach. *Anthropology and Education Quarterly, 12*(10), 3–29.

Poliner, R. A., & Lieber, C. M. (2004). *The advisory guide: Designing and implementing effective advisor programs in secondary schools.* Cambridge, MA: Educators for Social Responsibility.

Ryan, M. A. (2006). The role of social foundations in preparing teachers for culturally relevant practice. *Multicultural Education, 13*(3), 10–13.

Salahu-Din, D., Persky, H., & Miller, J. (2008). *The nation's report card: Writing 2007* (NCES 2008–468). Washington, DC: National Center for Education Statistics, Institute of Education Sciences, U.S. Department of Education, Washington, D.C. Retrieved from http://nces.ed.gov/pubsearch/pubsinfo.asp?pubid=2008468

San Pedro, T. J. (2011, April). Providing that "spark to know more" about ourselves: Implications of teaching Native American literature to Native American students. Paper Presented at the Annual Meeting of the American Educational Research Association, New Orleans, LA.

Scott, J. (2005). *The moments, the minutes, the hours: The poetry of Jill Scott.* New York: St. Martin's Press.

Shulman, L. S. (1987). Knowledge and teaching: Foundations of the new reform. *Harvard Educational Review, 57,* 1–22.

Siddle-Walker, E. V. (1992). Falling asleep and failure among African-American students: Rethinking assumptions about process teaching. *Theory into Practice, 31,* 321–327.

Weiss, J., & Herndon, S. (2001). *Brave new voices: The youth speaks guide to teaching spoken word poetry.* Portsmouth, NH: Heinemann.

Wilder, P. (2011). *Promoting student self-assessment* [Read WriteThink Strategy Guide]. Retrieved from http://www.readwritethink.org/professional-development/strategy-guides/promoting-student-self-assessment-30102.html

Winn, M. T. (2010a). "Betwixt and between": Literacy, liminality, and the celling of black girls. *Race, Ethnicity and Education, 13,* 425–447.

Winn, M. T. (2010b). "Our side of the story": Moving incarcerated youth voices from margins to center. *Race, Ethnicity and Education, 13,* 313–325.

Winn, M. T. (2011). *Girl time: Literacy, justice, and the school-to-prison pipeline.* New York: Teachers College Press.

Winn, M. T., & Ubiles, J. R. (2011). Worthy witnessing: Collaborative research in urban classrooms. In A. F. Ball and C. A. Tyson (Eds.), *Studying diversity in teacher education* (pp. 295–308). Lanham, MD: Rowman and Littlefield; Washington, DC: American Research Association.

Index

Authors

Maisha T. Winn is a former public elementary and high school teacher from Sacramento, California. Her ethnography, *Writing in Rhythm: Spoken Word Poetry in Urban Classrooms*, follows the lives of youth poets who use the spoken word as a tool to define themselves and chart their future lives. She is also the author of an ethnohistory of black readers, writers, and speakers of the Black Arts Movement entitled *Black Literate Lives: Historical and Contemporary Perspectives*. Her most recent book, *Girl Time: Literacy, Justice, and the School-to-Prison Pipeline*, examines the lives of formerly incarcerated girls who participate in a playwriting and performance program. Winn's research has been published in *Harvard Educational Review*; *Race, Ethnicity, and Education*; *Anthropology and Education Quarterly*; *Research in the Teaching of English*; *Written Communication*; and *English Education*. She is currently an associate professor of language, literacy, and culture in the Division of Educational Studies at Emory University.

Latrise P. Johnson attended Morris Brown College and served as a middle and high school English and writing teacher in Atlanta, Georgia, for six years. She is currently a PhD candidate in Emory University's Division of Educational Studies. Her dissertation focuses on the literacy practices of African American male youth, particularly the literacy ideologies, texts, and artifacts that complicate and/or extend notions of literate identities within and across in-school and out-of-school spaces. She is also director of a tutoring program for a local nonprofit organization that tutors students in reading, language arts, and mathematics. Johnson is currently one of NCTE's Cultivating New Voices Among Scholars of Color fellows (2010–2012 cohort).

This book was typeset in Janson Text and BotonBQ by
Barbara Frazier.

Typefaces used on the cover include American Typewriter,
Frutiger Bold, Formata Light, and Formata Bold.

The book was printed on 60-lb. Recycled Offset paper
by Versa Press, Inc.

30% Total Recycled Fiber